The
Polk Street Review

2018

Fact or Fiction?
YOU Decide . . .

The Polk Street Review
2018 edition
Fact or Fiction? YOU Decide . . .

Copyright © 2018 Logan Street Sanctuary, Inc.
Logan Street Sanctuary Press
1274 Logan Street
Noblesville, IN 46060
1st Printing
February 2018

Participating Authors, Photographers, Artists, and Musicians retain all copyrights to their material; all material used with permission.

Cover design: Alys Caviness-Gober
Cover art: *Star Bricks* (photograph): Alys Caviness-Gober
Logan Street Sanctuary Press team: Sarah E. Morin, Dr. Paul Wilson, Alys Caviness-Gober
Project management, formatting, and layout: Alys Caviness-Gober
Back cover design: Alys Caviness-Gober

Logan Street Sanctuary Press
Noblesville, IN
Copyright © 2018 Logan Street Sanctuary, Inc.
1274 Logan Street
Noblesville, IN 46060
loganstreetsanctuary.org

Paperback: ISBN-13: 978-0-9998858-1-9

The Polk Street Review
is always
dedicated to:
our community,
our friends,
and
our families.

Table Of Contents

Sponsors & Patrons

Indiana Arts Commission Arts Project Support

Logan Street Sanctuary, Inc. (LSS) gratefully thanks the *Indiana Arts Commission* for the FY2018 Region 7 Arts Project Grant received by LSS in support of the 2018 edition of *The Polk Street Review*.

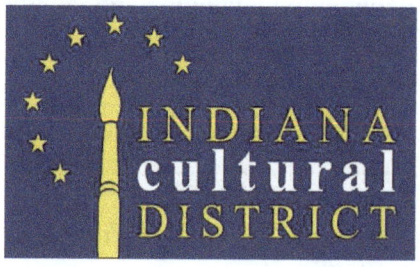

This activity made possible, in part, with support from the Indiana Arts Commission and the National Endowment for the Arts, a federal agency.

2018 Corporate Sponsors

Logan Street Sanctuary, Inc. gratefully thanks the following local businesses for their support of the 2018 edition of *The Polk Street Review*.

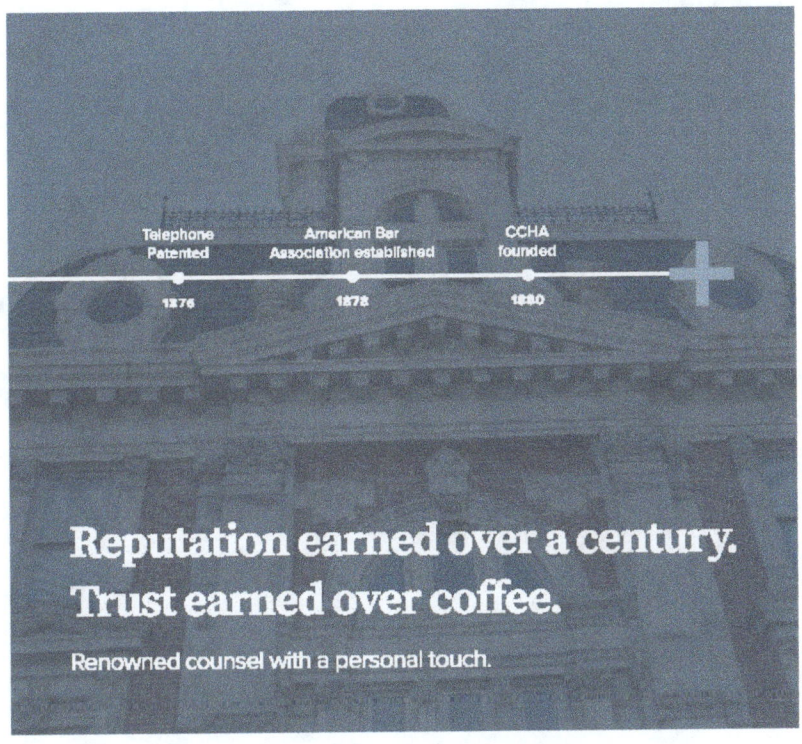

SMITH'S JEWELERS ON THE SQUARE

98 N. 9th Street

Downtown Noblesville

M-F 10-6, Sat 10-5

317.773.3383

www.smithonthesquare.com

Mr. G's Liquor offers quality service
along with a great selection of
wine, liquor, and beer
to Central Indiana residents.

Mr. G's was founded in 1977 in Noblesville, Indiana,
by Elijah, Wayne, and Myron Glover.
The store is now owned
by Myron and Bryan Glover.
The General Manager is Kirk Baird.

Mr. G's is proud to be associated with
all of the outstanding writers, photographers,
and artists that have contributed to
the 2017 edition of *The Polk Street Review*!

Our special thanks to
Logan Street Sanctuary, Inc.
for keeping this special publication
a part of the Noblesville Community!

Mr. G's is located at
2209 E. Conner St., Noblesville, IN 46060.
Telephone 317.773.3471
Website: mrgsliquors.com
Twitter: @mrgsliquors

2018 Individual Patrons

Logan Street Sanctuary, Inc. gratefully thanks the following individuals
for their support of
the 2018 edition of *The Polk Street Review*:

Bill & Casey Kenley
Emily Wasonga
Mark Wilkinson
Greg Richards
Matt & Kelli Yates
Luke & Sally Kenley
Kurt & Andrea Meyer
David & Laurie Kimmel
David & Stacy Corwin
Dottie & Vernon Young
Susan Crandall

Introduction

In February of 2017, *Logan Street Sanctuary* (LSS) launched its first publication of *The Polk Street Review* (TPSR). Immediately after the book launch event, I started preparing for the 2018 edition, and I do mean, immediately: right after we closed up LSS after the book launch, a few of us celebrated in TPSR's founding father Bill Kenley's kitchen. Riding the high of the book launch event, right then and there I came up with the 2018 theme: *Fact or Fiction? YOU Decide . . .* (with *YOU* being the reader). We all know the saying, *truth is stranger than fiction.* Think of how you feel when you wake up from a dream or nightmare so vivid that you aren't sure if it really happened or not. Or how you feel after having an experience that is so bizarre you know other people won't believe it really happened. For the 2018 edition, we asked for submissions that would leave our readers feeling unsure if what they'd read was fact or fiction. For artists and photographers, meeting this year's theme was a bit of a challenge, so we were generous with images insofar as connection to theme. A note about our ribbon awards: LSS Board Members, TPSR founding fathers Bill Kenley and Kurt Meyer, and family members of TPSR's editorial team are ineligible for awards, so this year, the ineligible include Sarah E. Morin, Spike Wilson, John Gilmore, Mike Stewart, John Caviness, Radka Caviness, and me. Also, only stand-alone images submitted specifically to the *Images* category are eligible for Awards; some images in the book are part of written submissions and do not qualify for awards.

Back to February 2017. I spent the next several weeks applying for grants (happily we received one, an *Indiana Arts Commission* Arts Project Grant), and Sarah E. Morin and I started prepping for the February 2018 publication date by scheduling workshops throughout 2017. Several entries herein are works created in those workshops.

It's a good thing we got so much done way back then, because March 2017 brought an overwhelming change to my year as my mother's health started to fail. LSS, *The Polk Street Review,* and most of my other responsibilities, projects, and interests fell by the wayside, as the two of us made a long, terrible, and final journey together. My tiny sweet mom, Radka Caviness, passed away in July of 2017.

Mom was the biggest fan of LSS, *The Polk Street Review*, and *NICE (Noblesville Interdisciplinary Creativity Expo)*. She loved this place that I call my home away from home; she loved that LSS took over publishing

The Polk Street Review, and she was thrilled to submit to the 2017 edition. She submitted her pieces to this 2018 book in late February 2017, right after last year's book launch. No surprise: Mom was the first person every year to submit to *NICE.* Last year, she had her 2017 *NICE* story-drawing memoir done way back in January of 2017, after I read to her our four chosen passages, before we even announced the passages publicly. She wrapped up her piece, asking me not to open it until the *NICE* event in October (2017).

After she passed away in July, I couldn't bring myself to unwrap it until the day before our *NICE* event last October. Her piece was inspired by our selected passage from *The Diary of Anne Frank;* it is my mom's take on the juxtaposition between the ideals upon which America was founded and the reality of America's Japanese Internment Camps during WWII. Her perspective was personal. Mom was born in Macedonia in 1939. She and her mother and sister immigrated to America in 1940 on the *Rex,* the last passenger ship out of Europe for the duration of WWII, and Mom grew up in Oregon, where the USA interred Japanese-Americans in camps. Those camps to her were far too much like the Nazi Concentration Camps in Europe. Most of Mom's relatives and family friends in Macedonia were killed in the War, either while fighting the Nazis or in the concentration camps.

Mom had a strong sense of human rights; I'm so proud of her last submission to *NICE.* I wish I had made her show it to me when she finished it, but she was like a little kid at Christmas, wanting me to wait until October. I wish I could have told her how much I love it, how it is so perfectly *her.* A poor substitute, but I've included in the *International Connection Section* of this book. We're also including a couple of my own *NICE* pieces here; a painting and a *tanka* poem that I created for my mom after she passed away. The inspiration for the poem and the painting come from something I experienced one day that fits this year's *The Polk Street Review* theme.

Saturday morning, July 8th, Mom insisted several times that I must go buy nectarines; she said they were her father's favorite fruit and we must have them "with him" for lunch (her father had passed away on my birthday in 1986). After breakfast, as I got her settled back into her bed, again she anxiously insisted that I go buy nectarines for lunch with her father. I promised I would, kissed her, and said I'd be right back. Off I went in search of nectarines.

The day was unbelievably lovely, not the normal stagnant stultifying humidity and heat of July in Indiana. It was warm but not hot, and there was a soft sweet breeze blowing. I found nectarines; when I exited the grocery store doors, a little yellow butterfly danced around me all the way to my car. I thought to myself, I *have to tell Mom about that happy little butterfly!* When I got back to my mom's house, I found she had passed away. I believe she was that dancing butterfly, letting me know she was happy and free from pain and illness.

I know she sent me on that errand to spare me being there when she passed. That was my mom. Both of us had always known that it would be me to find her, and I know that was a sorrow that weighed on her. If she could've spared me that moment, she would have.

In another *Fact or Fiction* moment, I found out later that, due to the Noblesville Street Dance, Randall & Roberts could not get from my mother's house on the south side of Noblesville to their facility out on St. Rd 32. They chose to take my mother's remains to their older Logan Street location. When they told me she would be there through the weekend, they were apologetic, as if not taking her directly to their other facility would be offensive to me. How could they now how perfect that twist of fate was, and how comforted I was, knowing she was resting near Logan Street Sanctuary, a place she truly loved.

In honor of my mother, we'd like to dedicate this volume to her life, her love, and her memory. Mom, this book is for you.

Alys Caviness-Gober
February 2018

Free
Alys Caviness-Gober

One of the oldest Japanese forms of verse, *tanka* originated in the seventh century. It is a thirty-one-syllable poem, traditionally written in a single unbroken line, but is better known in its five-line, 5/7/5/7/7 syllable count form. The *tanka* employs a turn, known as a pivotal image, which marks the transition from the examination of an image to the examination of the personal response. This turn is located within the third line, connecting the upper poem with the lower poem. Some of the most famous Japanese *tanka* poets were women. Among them was Lady Murasaki Shikibu, who wrote *The Tale of Genji*, a foundational Japanese prose text that includes over 400 *tanka*. *The Tale of Genji* was one of mother's favorite books, so I thought it appropriate to attempt a *tanka* for her, to go with my little painting. Here goes:

> a rare and sweet breeze
> on a bright July morning
> kissing my pale cheek
> and I hurry back to you
> as a butterfly dances

Free
Alys Caviness-Gober

The Polk Street Review
2018

Fact or Fiction?
YOU Decide . . .

Submission Categories:
Images
Song Lyrics/Poetry
Prose

International Connection Section

The Journey (How I Came To America)
Radka Caviness

Popche
Stavros A. (I only know the first letter of his long last name; we called him *Popche*, rather like some people call their grandfather *Pops* or *Poppy*.) He was born in Greece in 1896. He became Steve Adrian in America. His village and his family were desperately poor. In 1907, his mother showed him a ship, told him to stow away; the ship would take him to America. He always knew she did it because she loved him. He never blamed her.

The stowaway did not go to America. The ship took him to Argentina. He arrived in Argentina in 1907, eleven years old, penniless and alone. He knew "bad" men: child molesters. One of these men Stavros called a "good" man; the man helped him. Popche's odyssey to America took eight years. In 1915, he finally arrived in America, the dream realized. He worked with other immigrants laying railroad tracks for ten cents a day. He found the logging camps of Oregon. In an Oregon logging camp, he found Anto/Andrew/Grandpa. Steve learned to speak Macedonian. He had found the one person he never wanted to live without.

Grandpa
Anto Karstic was born in Tetovo, Macedonia, in 1898. In America, he became Andrew Karstic. Anto was my paternal grandmother's brother. He and his younger sister Fanka were orphaned and lived with their married sister Ana and her growing family. They were poor in a destitute place. Macedonia is landlocked, but Ana got him to a ship, told him to stow away; the ship would take him to America. He blamed her always.

The stowaway did not go to America. The ship took him to Argentina. Anto arrived in Argentina in 1908; ten years old, penniless and alone. His odyssey to America took nine years. He never spoke of his "bad" men. In 1917, he arrived in America, the promise realized. He worked with other immigrants laying railroad tracks for ten cents-a-day. He found the logging camps of Oregon. In an Oregon logging camp he found Stavros/Steve/Popche – the one person he never wanted to live without.

Steve and Andrew
In 1920, Prohibition (1920-1933) was their deliverance; their chance for a better life. They became hooligans, thugs – earning more and living in

Portland. I once asked Popche if he murdered people. He said, "You do whatever it takes, you do it all, kill or be killed."

Fanka

Fanka Karstic was born in Tetovo, Macedonia in 1902. In America, she became Fanka Adrian (we called her *Baba Fanka*). Fanka was my paternal grandmother's sister. She could never marry because the dowry left for her was needed by her sister Ana to feed and take care of Anto, my father, and the rest of Ana's family. Even as a child, Fanka was the old maid aunt, always beholden. She did chores and took care of Ana's children.

When Fanka was nineteen, her brother Anto delivered her from loneliness and servitude; he sent for her as a mail-order bride for his friend Steve. No one in Tetovo could believe it; they had not heard from Anto in all those years. They all thought Fanka had been born under a lucky star after all. Fanka arrived in Portland, Oregon, in 1921 and married Steve. She was nineteen years old. She understood nothing. Soon after the marriage, because of "female troubles" she was taken to a doctor who gave her a hysterectomy. 1921 was long before women's rights; she may have been legion.

Steve and Andrew catered to Fanka. They were like children who decide *if we act like she rules, and I call you names sometimes, then no one will guess the truth.* They had saved her from a miserable life in Macedonia. They gave her a comfortable empty life in America. She blamed them always.

Dad

Dushan Dimitri was born in Tetovo, Macedonia, on 03 August 1910. He was my father. In America, he became Dick Dimitri, then Dick Dimitrovich. He was the oldest of seven children. His family was not respected. They were considered uncouth and lazy and irresponsible. As the eldest son, he would always live with and provide for his parents, and his younger siblings until they married. Whomever he married would do all of the cooking and cleaning for his parents and siblings; such was Macedonian tradition. An eldest son's wife was destined to be a domestic slave.

As a child, Dushan worked part time at jobs found for him by his mother. He finished the ninth grade of school and then he had to work full time to support the family. Unlike the rest of his family, he was hardworking. He was handsome, popular, and a (poor-as-dirt) playboy. In Macedonia, marriages were arranged; no one would allow their daughter to marry into his disreputable family, let alone marry such a womanizer. When his required military service was over, Dushan's parents said he had to be married and they would find someone. They found Luba. At twenty-five, Dushan was considered an old groom.

Mama

Luba Samojlovski was born in Tetovo, Macedonia, on 16 September 1914. She is my mother. In America, she became Luba Dimitri, then Luba Dimitrovich. She was the third of seven children. Her family was respected. They were hardworking, well-mannered, and responsible. Luba finished the third grade of school. My mother had highly-prized blue eyes, despite the five-hundred-year conquest of Macedonia by the brown-eyed Turks. Macedonian Slavs were blond and blue-eyed before they were conquered.

Luba's blue eyes, and the fact that as a small child she survived being struck by lightning, endeared her to the local gypsies. They believed her to be chosen, favored by the gods; they adored her. To them, she was beautiful, special, magical. They took her. She adored them; they treated her like a princess and constantly told her how special, how beautiful, how wondrous she was. They kept her until she was about 15 years old. Then, they gave her back to her family; no one wanted their sons to marry her.

The two Macedonian families arranged a marriage between the womanizing man no one wanted their daughters to marry and the gypsy-tainted woman no one wanted their sons to marry. My mother and my father married on 17 November 1935. At twenty-one, she was considered a very old bride. My sister Olga was born in September 1936 and I was born in January 1939.

On an evening in 1986 when I was in Portland to spend time with my father, who was in the hospital recovering from surgery, I sat with my mother, my sisters Olga and Ana, my brother Stevie, having coffee together in our mother's garden. She told us this story:

Years before she married our father, she was engaged to a wealthy young man who was not from Tetovo. His parents came to Tetovo as marriage brokers, searching for a virgin, and found Luba. They gave her a necklace made of gold coins to seal the engagement. Her fiancé was mustered out of his compulsory military service a few days later and he came directly, still in his uniform, to meet her.

The moment he saw her, he was rude to her and her family, but she would not break the engagement. In Macedonia, the woman had to break the engagement, the man could not. He then hit her in the face and broke her nose. Still, she remained betrothed. Only when he set her family's house on fire did she relent. His parents insisted she keep the necklace. Our mother laughed and said: "He had to be crazy!"

Never underestimate the power of denial; we, her four children, looked at her speechless. We were thinking what Stevie finally said: "He wasn't crazy; he didn't *want* to marry you." We believed we knew why. Growing up in America in the Golden Age of Hollywood, we believed our mother was ugly. As an adult, I wish we had not thought that, I wish it had not colored our view of her even when we were adults.

1938
Fanka, Steve, and Andrew sent for my father's younger brother, Meso, twenty-three years old and unmarried. Two days before his departure, Meso was called up for his required military service. He turned to my father and said, "take my papers and you go." My father did.

When my father was a child, a gypsy told his fortune: "You will go across the big water to the golden place." He had never forgotten. He knew it was written in the stars. At last, he was going to America; it was the great escape, from poverty, from his family, from his wife, from fatherhood. He arrived in Portland, Oregon, on 08 April 1938. He was twenty-seven years old. He was a surprise to his uncle and his aunt and Steve, who expected Meso, but my father was deliriously happy. He was free.

1940
Fanka, Steve, and Andrew paid for my mother, Olga, and myself to come to America. We believed our father had sent for us. Our mother had her deliverance. She had been born under a lucky star after all. We traveled by train to Genoa, Italy, and left on the *REX*, the last passenger ship to leave Europe for the duration of the Second World War. We left in the spring of 1940. My sister Olga remembered leaving; she remembered the sound of the German bombs. We arrived in Portland, Oregon, on 08 May 1940.

My mother had never seen the ocean, but she had to cross it. My mother knew nothing of America, but she had to cross it. My mother had not seen her husband for almost two years since the spring of 1938, but she was pregnant. In the month of May 1940, in this new world, my mother went to an eye doctor and was given glasses, she went to a dentist and was given false teeth, and she went to a back-alley quack and was given an abortion.

Olga remembered our sad welcome at the train station in Portland. Our father was there with his life-long best friend, George (eight years younger than Dushan, he was brought to America by his aunt Simoitza). Our father never got out of George's car. We went in Fanka, Steve, and Andrew's car to our new life. My father, mother, sister, and I lived with them for the next two years and our father continued to work long hours in their tavern.

As children, we were aware that our father didn't like us or our mother, that he seemed to resent us and was unkind. We understood nothing; why he sent for us, why he married our mother.

The Second World War changed everything. Dad worked in the Swan Island shipyards during the war, then with a painting company, briefly had a tavern with George, had his own painting company (again briefly) and then returned to the shipyards, joining the painters union. He was one of the small crew of maintenance and repair workers for the ships and freighters that come to the Swan Island shipyard. Twenty years later, in 1975, he retired. In 1942, we moved into our own rented apartment. It was an old house in Southeast Portland, divided into two apartments and owned by successful Macedonian immigrants, Yordana and Vasil Majovski. My father bought a house in 1947; the American dream realized.

In 1943, changes were being made in draft eligibility. Married men with two children could be drafted. Our father decided to have another child. My sister Ana was born. Ana was named for both grandmothers. Eight years later, my mother refused an abortion and my brother Stevie was born; he was named for Popche. Olga and I were always perplexed; we were named for no one.

1986
From Indiana, I went to visit my father in a Portland hospital. He had terminal colon cancer. I visited him each day, always taking my mother in the mornings and returning without her in the afternoons, when George

and others drop by. One morning, my mother said she would go in the afternoon, so I went alone.

My father told me of his great happiness when he arrived in America. He happily worked in Fanka, Steve, and Andrew's tavern for no wages, only some spending money. On his days off, he went downtown to stroll around and go to the movies. He felt young and free. His life was beautiful. Then his Aunt Fanka began to say he could not go anywhere on his day off. She wanted him to stay home and spend time with her. He had to do what she said or, she said, HE WOULD BE SORRY.

My father told me: "I didn't pay any attention to her. What can she do to me? Nothing. Boy, I sure found out. She did something I never dreamed she could do. She brought your mother and Olga and you to America. You were my punishment. In Tetovo, I loved a girl I could never marry; her parents would never allow it. In America, I loved another girl, Bertha. She asked me if I had lost my mind, and why was I bringing my family? I told her I am not bringing them. They are coming and I cannot stop it. I was stuck with my punishment."

We had seen Bertha over the years at *Podkrepa*, our Macedonian Social Club. She was a lovely rich American-born Macedonian, and I understood finally that my father had not had anything he wanted. He was not the first immigrant to escape a family he never wanted: to come to America reborn and free. He was legion.

That he had not sent for us was an unexpected and stunning revelation. The child I was had felt his rejection, his sometimes fury, and his unmelting heart. I wish the child-me had known the truth. The truth does set you free.

My father's punishment was long and severe and true, but it was not for him alone; he shared it with us.

My mother, my sister Olga, and I came to the golden place, not because a gypsy said we would; we came to the golden place because my Baba Fanka said we would. She gave us our deliverance from hardship and poverty and peril. I always loved her, and now I thank her always.

They all believed in fate and the stars, the evil eye and hexes, in werewolves and vampires, and God. They were ignorant and wise. They lived their strange lives. They were all heroes.

Church Window
Gail Geisler

At the Ancient Ferret Chapel, La Fouly, Switzerland.

Reflections
Gail Geisler

Reflections from Bosnia
Gail Geisler

In my beautiful country
There was a time
When we were neighbors and friends
And then we weren't

The man at the newsstand
Where I went every week
To get my uncle's cigarettes
Stopped smiling at me, demanding

Bosniak or Serb?
I was nine years old
And I couldn't answer
Because I'd never had to choose

My childhood ended
When the snipers began
I saw the fear in my parent's eyes
I watched my brother die

Four years of terror
Every day hungry and afraid
One hundred ten thousand
Slaughtered

Bosniak or Serb? Allah or Jesus?
One hundred ten thousand
Slaughtered
In my haunted country

I watched my brother die
And I stopped smiling
Four years of terror
In my parent's eyes

Then it stopped
And we were supposed to return
To a mythical time
When we were neighbors and friends

Immigrant Family 1700
Vivian Belle

Came we three
across the sea
to be free;

our family
mère, père, bébé
firstborn Henrí;

from France to Wales
through Ireland's gales
our ship sails;

freedom found
this hallowed ground
Amen resound;

from the dock
in freedom we walk
with freedom we talk;

dream achieved
forever relieved
or so we believed.

From Henrí to me
a line enduring;
are we still free?

Caution
Gail Geisler

A far too realistic fake construction worker inside a tunnel along SS145 near Castellammare, Italy between Pompeii and Sorrento.

Through the door, floor, and sky
John Caviness

Deep into that darkness peering, long I stood there, wondering, fearing, doubting, dreaming dreams no mortal ever dared to dream before. – Edgar Allan Poe

I awoke, dirty and confused. My surroundings were that of a semi-abandoned mall, wherein hundreds upon thousands of some currency lay cast on the ground, covering up dirty tiles. These strange bank notes were everywhere. There were strange advertisements on the windows of closed businesses, none with real words on them, but they were comprised of bizarre shorthand, with word combinations that were simultaneously oddly familiar and foreign. My mind raced with confusion.

While venturing through this mall, I ran into people, all with a squalid look like the one I noticed on myself when I caught a glimpse of my image in the glare of a shop window. Some of the people addressed me, most often only quickly telling me to get out of the way. Others simply kept to themselves, but looked at me with wild eyes, searching for something but not finding it.

The lights were on inside this deserted mall, at least what bulbs still worked. It was so desolate. This environment forced me into feeling that I needed to leave, fearing for what may become of me if I stayed. In looking for the exit, I saw more businesses, one looking like a phone carrier, one seeming to be a looted electronics store, inside which there were no electronics, only decrepit people sleeping.

Finally, I found a door, an exit, and walked through it. I noticed something immediately. There should have been sunlight, or the glow of the moon, but instead there was an artificial glow outside.

All I could think was, *What is this place?* It wasn't part of my familiar German town. As I made my way through the strangely lit door, the sight I saw was something out of a nightmare. Societal collapse. A sort of poverty I couldn't believe, which seemed to be the remnants of a bloated and cruel system that appeared to be long gone, but still impacted the living. Huddled, depressed people, all grouped up in small cliques, near a corner sheltering themselves from the rain, which fell lightly but starkly enough to dampen their clothes and chill their skin. I glanced upward, to see the sky and clouds, and only saw suspended roads and enormous buildings. The buildings were highly technologically advanced, like Nar Shaddaa in *Star Wars*, but this place wasn't a movie set – it was not the German city I live in, it didn't even seem like planet Earth, but rather a shell of it.

I drew my hood up on my crusty jacket, which apparently I hadn't washed in quite some time. The rain felt nice, and I welcomed it as I explored this strange land. I came across a part of town, similar to a place down the street from where I live (a place that is a beautiful park, even though the abundance of drug abusing junkies riddling the place detracts from the natural beauty it holds). But here, in *this* place, the ones on this plot of land, were frantically pulling from electronic tubes, much like E-Cigs. Instead of vapor, when they exhaled out came a vile neon green gas, and their subsequent coughing was loud, louder than that of the traffic I could hear, yet couldn't see. I didn't dare talk to one of them, but then one approached me, asking in a strange language for a 20,000 Bank Note.

I looked at him, looked down, and said. "Start picking up twenties, brother, I don't have any." I knew and spoke the language somehow, which surprised me. He spat on my uncovered feet, with a fetid slobber that was green like the gas, and left. I continued walking; it felt like I walked for hours, until I came across a cart, open with the cartridges and tubes that I had seen people using at the park.

A man was standing on top of it shouting, "Refills, 20,000. New Units 50,000!"

My head couldn't fathom the people around me, and how they could afford the drug and its paraphernalia, even though the ground was paved in ruddy, soggy bank notes. After thinking that he was looking at me like I might steal from his cart, I ran. Somehow, in my escape, someone pulled me into a building. It seemed I knew her, but at the same time, I didn't know her. I couldn't make out her face in the dim lighting, and her voice was so low as to not draw attention.

"John," she said, "What are you doing here? You should be far from here."

Just as the lights grew brighter, and the face became more clear . . . the scene shifted drastically. I felt no control over the what was happening; I am not filtering anything out of what I experienced, despite the qualms I have with sharing what happened. The holes in my story stem from what my memory no longer can recall.

As her face came into vision, I noticed that I was falling. Literally falling down, directly into a hole that appeared in floor beneath my feet. I fell for what seemed like seconds, but in slow motion, and as I fell, all I could think to say is, *Who are you?! Why am I in this awful place?! Where am I going!?* My mouth uttered nothing, and I fell deeper and deeper through this bizarre world and landed in another.

There is something they don't tell you about weightlessness. It hurts like hell; the human body is made for simple movements and adaptation over eons of time. When it comes to sudden change, the human body doesn't respond painlessly.

I found myself falling into a blue sky. Bluer than a clear lake, with white fluffy clouds enveloping a beautiful landscape, speckled with plants and blooming flowers and lush trees. As I fell, I took in the landscape and saw that in the middle of my field of vision rose a large mountain. Around this mountain, an expansive body of crystal-clear water lay still, and a small quiet-looking town was nearby. In a flash I saw a green vapor descending from the Mountain-top, approaching this beautiful place; I knew the desolation that was coming. Then I landed hard and fell asleep; my body reacting to what just happened.

How long I slept, I do not know, but I awakened to crashing sounds, and the strangest thing had happened to me: the ruddy clothes I'd had on before were replaced with modernized armor. Now, my attire was Kevlar and military-style khakis. In the distance I heard shouting and crashing. The trees around me were tiny, but I wasn't even standing.
Upon standing, I could see the town was still in view, as was a horrible monster spewing his fetid green breath into the pure air.

They say Godzilla is the king of all Monsters, and that he is the Defending Spirit of the Mountain from where he comes; I thought of that when I first saw the creature. He was no defending spirit, he was the opposite. Maliciously, he laid waste to parts of the town, occasionally snatching up people and slowly chewing them up and eating them. I ran to them, hoping to save them, but by the time I covered the distance, I couldn't see any other people. There was no one left, other than me and the Godzillian Behemoth before me.

Then began our fight for the Mountain, like a real-life battle of the playground game, King of the Hill. I never knew myself to be a fighter, nor to be as tall as a fifteen-story monster. I realized that when one is presented with a foe of such stature, something primal kicks in; perhaps an instinct to survive or a macho desire to conquer something so ostensibly unconquerable, I don't know. Whatever it was, kicked in and we came to blows in a battle I could never have imagined. The creature emitted terrifying monster-screams of rage, and I heard my own voice shouting out battle-cries like those of warriors in movies, fighting to the death. The Behemoth and I swiped away at each other, my red blood mingling with his green blood upon the earth.

At one point, through my bloodied peripheral vision, I saw the monster's razored teeth unavoidably close as he bit into my shoulder, but I somehow managed to pull his jaws apart and lift him by them, and fling him towards the Mountain. He got back up, seemingly unscathed; equally oddly, my shoulder felt fine. Confusion swirled in my head as I realized that neither of us actually suffered from our wounds; *A battle where wounds do not manifest?* Although I was glad that my wounds were not killing me, I was not comforted. *How do I beat him?* That single thought blared through my mind.

I tackled him to the ground, and we rolled around, nearer and nearer to the water, exchanging the upper hand, each wounding the other, when eventually we rolled to the lakeside. He put my head under; I never felt so scared before. Suddenly his grip loosened slightly, and I twisted him from above me, and kicked him into the water. Roaring with rage, he sank; either he could not swim or his weight took him under. I neither knew, nor cared, why he sank, but I did wonder, *Why had he loosed his grip?* I thought he was indeed defeated, but how does one know when a Monster really is dead?

As I turned my back, he grabbed my leg, and pulled me into the water.

If there is one thing anyone who really knows me knows, it is that I am an awful swimmer. However, in this fight, swimming was actually easier than standing. I struggled to find something with which kill the beast. About 15 monster-paces from where we were fighting, there was a mammoth stone wall at the edge of the lake, a wall upon which a huge rock precariously rested. I slowly began moving towards the wall, while spinning and spiraling with my opponent.

My determination did not wane, but I was beginning to feel at least one effect of our battle: exhaustion. The kind of exhaustion where your muscles feel like wet noodles. As we neared the wall, the monster had me pinned underwater. I could see the wall and the rock, shimmering above me through the clear lake water. Burbling bubbles of what seemed my last breath escaped me as I used my remaining strength to throw him up off me and into the wall.

Water doesn't carry sound, but I felt the vibration of my final battle-cry as the creature slammed into the wall. The impact caused the rock to fall, crushing him down into the lake just as I simultaneously broke through the surface. I will never forget the look in that monster's eyes as he saw the rock coming down upon him, or the subsequent bone-crushing sounds that followed.

Worn out, I made it back to shore, dragged myself out of the lake and began walking towards the Mountain. Mentally, despite my exhaustion, I prepared for the ascent up the Mountain. My hope upon reaching the summit was that it might give me some bearing as to where I was, and even perhaps who I was; the John I know myself to be cannot swim well enough to survive that water-battle, or skydive through mysterious floor-doors into blue skies, nor does he go toe-to-toe in physical fights with people (let alone monsters) and then manage to best them. Who would I find myself to be, at the top of that mountain? What would I see? I climbed on.

When I reached the top, I gazed out onto that beautiful landscape, and saw that there was no desolation, no green-vapor destitution. I stood there for what felt like years . . . and I saw the town come back to life. I saw the people, so small in the distance, live out their lives. I watched them, I watched from my mountain-top view as people were born, grew up, played, worked, married, had children; I watched generation after generation live. Peacefully, I watched, like Godzilla, Defending Spirit of the Mountain. All the while I waited for the next sequence of events to occur, for the unexpected rush through a door or a floor into another sky where I would awaken into another strange world.

When nothing came to pass, I closed my eyes . . . and when I awoke again, I was in Germany, back in my bed and just a little chilly from the open window. I was both confounded and relieved to find myself in a familiar world, and I arose to go about my ordinary day, grateful for a break in my tempestuous adventures.

Falling Through The Cracks
Gail Geisler

In Plitvice National Park, Croatia.

The Great State of Canada

Jenny Kalahar
Tie for *First Place*, Prose Category

Growing up, I had always suspected that I'd had an ancestor who'd fought in the CanAm War of 1902-1905, but my father would only get a certain look in his eye when I brought up the topic. Now that we live in the age of the internet, and since I'd had a question from my son about our family's military past, I decided to do some online research.

Sitting down in front of my monitor with a cup of chocolate milk one predawn morning, still in my yellow bathrobe, I logged onto the genealogy site I'd recently joined. In the general history section, I refreshed my knowledge of that war, surprised again at just how many casualties there had been on both sides. Canada had suffered losses estimated to be nearly seventy percent of all its soldiers, and twenty percent of civilians. The northern territories were nearly uninhabited in 1905 except for Inuit and Metis peoples. Canada had drained its resources dry by the end of the first half of that last year of the war, causing widespread starvation across the land. There had been so many small skirmishes in so many remote locales that when the war had ended it took nearly seven months for word to entirely spread. The U.S. declared that Canada should henceforth be known as the 25th state, and supplies were immediately sent to northern cities and settlements. Shipments of aid were sent for two full years, until settlers from the lower states had farms producing reliably again, and wild land had been cleared for town growth. Schools were quickly erected, and churches, merchant buildings and more were built in designated areas. Theodore Roosevelt established national parklands and protected waterways from what he termed "unstable damming plans". Cries of "Head north! Head north! Sow your sparkling seeds!" were heard throughout the lower twenty-four states, and were printed in each major newspaper for several months after the war ended. Mining was a major industry, as was processing minerals and their byproducts.

It all seemed, from what the genealogical site stated, like we'd rescued Canada from itself. There was nothing written of just how well or how poorly Canadians were faring before 1902. Nothing of what had provoked this war in the first place. Land greed? Roosevelt's yearning for more natural resources? None of that seemed likely, given that our own westward expansion still had so very much promise.

I then searched my family tree on my father's side. Once I'd found my two-times great Grandpa Manard's middle name, the details and information on his life overwhelmed me! Manard Botell Rogers was an assistant surveyor under doctor and explorer John Rae. He'd taught Rae many skills of living off the land, hunting, boat-handling, and snowshoe navigation. It was Rae who took credit for most of the discoveries that Rogers had, in actuality, made.

When he was an old man retired to an Ontario farm, Rogers discovered, quite by accident, that the soil around small streams near his home was colored an unusual shade of blue. Even the fish swimming delicately in those streams were tinted blue, no matter their species. He bottled the waters and soils and hand-delivered them to a physician friend who had access to the laboratories of the University of Toronto. The substance was then unknown, but it is what we today call phosphorteem, the world's most expensive mineral. It was tested and shown to give off a bright light for up to twenty hours after being compressed even slightly. It has the ability to both store and emit energy. It is a deadly poison to humans if ingested or rubbed on the skin, but it is a miracle mineral for the new age! And that, undoubtedly, was what Roosevelt wanted to claim for the United States. That was the true reason for the war.

I relaxed against the back of my wooden chair, scowling. So, was my ancestor a hero, or was he the root cause of so much turmoil and death, famine and destruction? I thought about phosphorteem, then. It was powering everything in my house, my autocraft, and my own internal joint mechanisms within their titanium sheaths. It had been the answer to the coal smoke pollution problem that had hurt our atmosphere at the turn of the last century. Now the air is clean, the water pure, and the trees a lovely shade of brown – all thanks to my ancestor's discovery of that blue mineral.

I shrank my computer screen and placed it back into my robe's pocket. I would never know just how much had been affected by that stroll along a stream that my great-great grandfather had taken in early 1902, but something told me that life on Earth would have been very different had some other explorer thought of the blue soil as merely an anomaly in that part of Ontario. Or, perhaps, maybe it would have been scientifically tested decades later, long after other wars tore our countries apart or led to the destruction of Europe and Africa. Like that proverbial flap of a butterfly's wings causing the poles to shift and dinosaurs to become instinct, the world without this discovery can never fully be imagined.

Magic Mushroom
Gail Geisler
Tie for *Second Place*, Images Category

Along the Tour du Mont Blanc trek between Les Houches and Les Contamines, France.

Huguenot Cross
Vivian Belle

Hope
Jenny Kalahar

We each took a last swallow of the sand-colored, thick concoction made of grain collected from silos on an abandoned farm in Michigan that hot, airless night.

"Pass me the jar, will ya?" asked Pa.

We all called the old bent man *Pa*, but he'd only joined us a few weeks ago on our trek along an interstate highway leading to Detroit.

"All empty," said Arf, the boy who, until recently, had only barked and panted when speaking. He was hollow and traumatized — like all of us. Everyone had their own way of expressing their trauma, or of keeping it suppressed.

The water we found where we could was probably the equivalent of a slow-acting poison, and its taste was pure nightmare. Adding grain to it at least made it something we could tolerate.

Barney John lit a candle stub and wedged the hunk of white wax into a wide gap in the floorboards of the barn where we twelve adults and three kids huddled. That single source of light was enough for me. I didn't want to see my friends' faces clearly. We were soiled, ragged, nearly naked, and nearly ghosts.

"What will we do if we don't find the conditions any better in Canada, Pa?" asked Jamie.

Weak, thin-voiced Jamie had finally cut off almost all of her matted brown hair the night before. I hadn't totally lost my sense of humanity; I was still trying to keep my private parts covered with the rags I wore, and I still combed my short, dirty blond hair every morning. I wore the black plastic comb like a holstered gun in my waistband, and felt it protecting me from the unseen monsters of my mind.

We spoke the word "Canada" as if we were saying an ancient name for the Promised Land. Surely the death and destruction from the Troubles hadn't crossed national borders. Right?

Patch stretched her bare, tanned legs out across the floor and placed her rough, calloused feet onto my lap. I massaged them absentmindedly. This was now our nightly habit. Patch suffered with every step. No one had shoes except Pa. Almost everyone had run from houses and apartments in the middle of the night six months before. No one wanted to take them off the corpses, and there were none left to steal from deserted shops.

"Ma?" Patch asked me. "Did you used to be pretty?"

I concentrated on rubbing her left heel and said, "No. I was always plain. My eyes are my only –"

"Oh, yes!" she interrupted as I switched to rubbing her right foot. "I can't look enough at your blue eyes. Tell me again how you got to be 'Ma,' please."

I didn't smile at any sense of flattery at her invitation to repeat the story. I smiled because she needed me to. "I'm the oldest lady, that's why. Not that thirty-seven is so very old, you know. I was wandering alone for nearly a month before I found Barney John leaning against a small town's bookstore window. He was reading *Little House on the Prairie*. He was so startled to see another living person that the first word out of his mouth was 'Ma.' It stuck. Funny – being Ma to you lot makes me only four years older than my first-born."

The group made themselves comfortable for the night on the scattered piles of hay. Pa took out his harmonica and played a sleep-tight tune, the low notes reverberating around the big, mildewy barn and around the empty spaces in our hearts.

A soft rain woke us in the morning. I looked at Patch's feet in the better light of day and felt renewed shock at their condition. Making a decision, I took off what remained of my shirt and tore it in half. She would have some protection from the road, even if it did mean that I lost more of my modesty. No one said a word, but Pa's eyes teared up as he watched me tie the red cloth strips securely around Patch's feet.

A week later, Canada stretched promisingly just across Ambassador Bridge after we'd passed through countless horrors of what remained of our last American city. We'd slept inside an empty semi-truck at its Detroit side, not daring to cross on a moonless night. I dreamed of finding a department store off the highway where there would perhaps be clothing for all of us, but I knew reaching Canada was more important than covering my bare skin.

Rachel, a stick-thin woman of about twenty-five, screamed in horror when she first got out of the truck and saw clearly where we had been sleeping. The bridge was enormous to us all. We were all shaking and hugging, but I couldn't calm down Rachel.

Finally, she was able to say what was frightening her. "On the way here there was still the hope of Canada. Now … what if it's just the same? Will we have Peter hunt moose for us to eat with the canned food instead of deer and rabbit? Will the Canadian water still burn our insides? What if it's just the same, Ma?"

"Let's get there first before asking more questions." I turned to look at everyone slowly, making my words orders. "Don't look inside the cars. Don't look inside the cars, anyone!" I called. That was always the rule as we'd traveled the highway, but I wanted to say it again before we crossed.

Patch clung closely to me on the walk over the river, and Pa took the lead. It took forever, it felt like, and, since I have a fear of heights, the bridge's elevation kept a scream constantly boiling at the back of my throat.

As we neared the end, a large highway sign had been turned over and leaned against a SUV. On it had been spray-painted: "No hope here, but welcome home."

Everywhere we looked were people! Worn down and thin, but happy. We were the newest to cross over – all Americans who had hoped things might be different on the other side of that bridge. And maybe they were. I don't know how many men, women and children I embraced in those first minutes, my breasts still uncovered, but it may have been a hundred. We ate canned food and drank filtered water. A nurse in a makeshift medical center in an old pharmacy cared for Patch's feet in ways we couldn't have. We were all clean and wearing new clothing by suppertime.

Maybe we'd all survive together, and maybe we wouldn't. Maybe the poisons of the water we'd drunk for months would take effect in a day or a week and I would be 'Ma' no more. But we had crossed the bridge together and we had what we'd been seeking, despite the declaration of that sign. We had hope.

Home Sweet Home

Radka Caviness

Fact or Fiction?
YOU Decide . . .

She Still Shines

Annie Oberman

Quiet anticipation builds
As she takes the stage
A still, steady light
Surrounded by a sea of darkness
She breathes in this moment
Bow lifted, Spirit-gifted
It's time to begin
Gentle gliding
Strings abiding
As her song echoes
Through the sanctuary
Like a river flowing
Winter song snowing
The soft melody piercing
Unsuspecting hearts
Enchanted beauty beckoning
Each measure brimming with hope
As she nears the consummation
With one last breath
Long and steady
Satisfaction smiling
She takes a bow
Applause erupting
And the dance
In the darkness
Is finished
And yet still
She shines.

For the Love of Violin
Annie Oberman

House of Dreams

Vivian Belle
Tie for *First Place*, Prose Category

Old houses groan and creak at night. Like an old person settling into bed, their foundations settle and resettle, the old planks adjust, crackling and snapping under their own weight. An old house's infirmities are invisible and silent during the daytime.

From the outside, my house is perfection, the house of my dreams. It stands gently among the Spanish Moss-draped pines, honeysuckles, wisteria, magnolias, and roses surround it in a fragrant and colorful embrace. The old porch beckons. I fell in love with it when I saw it, my forebears' plantation home, my southern belle. It had taken me a while to find it, but I'd enjoyed the hunt, the research, and that final moment of setting eyes on it for the first time was priceless. Imagine seeing that for the very first time: the land where my family first had settled, the house that they built, the house in which they lived, loved, laughed, were born and died. My family lived there for over a hundred years, sometimes three or four generations under the same roof at once. In turn neglected and renovated over the years, it had changed hands many times, eventually passing to others for another hundred years or so. I dreamed I would hunt it down and bring it back into our family. When finally I found it and bought it, my dreams came true.

Old houses, like mine, have history; just like people, their own genealogy of owners and experiences. Even the land they sit on has history, echoes of the time before the building. . . .

"Stealth, my son."

The deer before them stood still, as if it was waiting for them. He knew that was his imagination; the deer was waiting for them, was not even sensing their presence. His father had taught him well – no one could get as close as his father, the best and bravest in the village. Imperceptibly, in unison, they raised their bows, took aim, and felled the deer. So silent, so swift were their arrows that it was as if the deer fell on its own, by magic.

Suddenly, the stillness of his father changed. The boy sensed a rigidity, and waited for his father to move forward to their kill. It would feed many. His father's face turned, away from the deer, away from their hunt.

"Come," the father said.

For a moment, the boy did not move, but in a flash-second he felt the hair on the back of his neck rise, and in the same moment his stomach fell; such was his father's tone.

Never had his father moved so swiftly; they ran as if on fire through the woods. The path was unfamiliar to the boy, not the way they had come, yet his father melted into the forest before him. Time passed. Miles passed under their feet. The boy could barely keep up, his exhaustion made his legs feel as weak as young willow branches, but it was as if he were bound to his father's body with an invisible tether. His father's urgency pulled him forward, unrelentingly through the forest.

With no warning, his father stopped, one leg raised in mid-step. The boy slammed into his father's back and they both jerked forward awkwardly, but his father's arm stopped the boy's momentum. The boy looked up questioningly and in the same moment, smelled it. Never had he smelled such a smell.

They moved forward again, slowly this time, the dread on his father's face seemed to move through them as if they were one, down to their feet. The boy felt the earth beneath his feet, like he had felt it all his life, but now the earth was different. They followed no path, but circled and circled slowly spiraling forward through the thick brush of the woods. With twisted and uncharacteristic movement, his father's arm kept him one step back, and the boy felt his father's grip on his shoulder, holding him in place, almost pushing him backwards as they moved warily forward.

The grip tightened on his shoulder. "Do not move," came his father's voice, spoken directly into his ear, so quiet he almost thought it was his imagination at work again. One more squeeze on his shoulder told him it was not. His father disappeared through the brush. The boy stood, waiting.

The smell was stronger, a burnt smell, but more than burnt. Dread filled him. He detected the smell of burnt wood and straw, horseflesh and hide, even the smell of burnt dog. But another smell was unknown, and he knew it was something terrible. Vomit surged from his stomach and he bent, retching.

The boy's body went cold and he shivered, sweat dripped down his back and brow. The sounds of the forest seemed to undulate, first the common sounds of insects and small animals magnified, then receded, then magnified, then receded. Sun dappling through the pine treetops stabbed his eyes. A twig snapped loudly.

Slowly, he disobeyed his father. He lowered his eyes to the earth, to the spot where his father had moved forward through the thickness of the forest. The boy's training kicked in, and he followed his father's path; no other man alive could have followed his father, but he could.

Minutes later, he was at the edge of the clearing, the far edge of their village, opposite their home. His eyes had no need to adjust from the shadowy forest; a thick dark haze stung his eyes, a haze gently drifting, similarly shrouding his vision.

In a moment, his brain took in the scene, the still-burning mounds of log and thatch and mud that had been homes, blackened trunks and branches of once-fragrant trees and bushes, the smoldering animal remains.

Without realizing it, he walked further, barely aware of the cinders and ashes under his feet. All was destroyed. All was burning, flames still licking in the smoldering heaps. His tearing eyes fell upon a burned lump; the remains of a person – *who is it?* his brain asked. No way to know; just a lump of blackened flesh and bone. He realized they were everywhere, these lumps, these human carcasses burnt and twisted. His friends. His village. They were the unknown smell.

Dread solidified in his heart.

He saw his father ahead, bent and kneeling. Once before had he seen his father on his knees, three summers ago when his baby sister was born and their father knelt by their mother's side to hold her for the first time. Now, his father's arms were outstretched, as if to receive a newborn child into his embrace. Below his father's hands, just under them, lay a small burnt body, just beyond lay a larger one with what was once an arm outstretched to the small body. The boy knew; the charred lumps were his baby sister and mother. They were black and unrecognizable but he knew.

His father's hands trembled just above his sister's body, as though perhaps some force could descend from them and imbue life. As the boy came near, his father's head turned towards him. Eyes and mouth open wide, a silent scream heard only inside each other's heads came from his father's throat.

In the darkness, I awake. My house awakens with me. History shudders and the ghosts come. There are two that move with unbelievably stealth to my bedside.

Now I know: they were always waiting for me.

I've tried to get away, I've tried other rooms. Night after night, the doors and windows keep me in. At first, I thought I was dreaming, the doors and windows open freely in the daylight; why can I not open them at night? Each morning, I wonder – *was I sleepwalking when I tried to escape?*

I've tried to sell, but no one buys. No one even comes to look; my house is invisible on the market. Thus, I have is no sanctuary; they find me, with the same silent deadliness as when they found the deer. It is not sleepwalking, it is not dreaming, it is not a deep nightmare of the slumbering mind, but a waking nightmare of a living eternity.

Every night, my house awakens with a silent scream that only I can hear, and they come, the ghostly shades of a boy and a man, they come with stealth and hatred. They stand silent, they stand so still, as my bed burns. They watch as I am engulfed in flames, as my brain boils, and my limbs twist from the heat. In horror and in unrelenting pain I scream, I beg, I pray. They stand, deaf to my pleadings and my screams, which we three hear only in our minds. The silence is unreal yet real. We three alone hear the fire crackle and consume, we three alone witness my destruction night after night.

They watch in silence, as their vengeance completes.

Author's Note:
I wrote down this living nightmare in 2012. It is now 2018. My house is still for sale.

Farmers Market Flowers: Perspective
Kathryn Anderson
Tie for *Second Place*, Images Category

In *The Polk Street Review* workshop for photography, I realized perspective really matters: is the bouquet being given to someone, or were they given to the person holding them? YOU decide!

Theory
DeMaris Gaunt

Maybe the saddest
and most bittersweet
realization in life
is that we don't stay broken
that we heal, we recover
from the love we thought
could never end
and that love can be replaced
which means we were wrong
it means we misjudged
the function of our hearts
which was never
to stay in one place
but to keep searching
for a source to fill
what will never be full.

Jimmy and the Stingray Summer

Greg Richards

Honorable Mention, Prose Category

This tale I've been thinking about is based on an event that occurred on a summer day fifty years ago, give or take a few. Now… while I accept that our memories slightly alter themselves each time we recollect them, I also believe that these constantly evolving memories remain factual to us, who are the characters within and the carriers of these ever-changing internal short films. Throughout our lives we re-forge these narratives every time they resurface and we think or talk about them. Writing is our best chance for giving these memories some degree of solidity, some hope for permanence. What I will tell you now about what happened on North Pillsbury Street that summer back then will be mostly true… *mostly*. And I'll fabricate from fragments of memories what I can't accurately recall of the rest of the story that played out during my stingray summer.

The long-defunct railroad still splits my home town from north to south with a rusty side-track at the grain elevator in the middle of town and another at the canning factory, also defunct, on the south end of town. State Highway 244 splits it east and west. The population of each of these quadrants of Milroy, Indiana, is roughly the same – that is if you count the citizens in the cemetery just outside town in the southeast quarter. The 2010 census says that 291 males and 313 females exist in my hometown. I'll take their word for it. I moved away after high school and seldom return, though it is a peaceful little town and was an adventurous world for kids growing up mid-twentieth century. Not much has changed. People don't build new houses in small rural towns anymore. Though the population of my hometown has little to do with my story, its layout is significant. Boys on bikes in summer "live or die" by their knowledge of the hills, gravel, short cuts, maple tree roots pushing up chunks of sidewalk, and all the topography of their small-town worlds. My hometown of Milroy, Indiana, was my Lake Wobegon; my Winesburg, Ohio; my Yoknapatawpha County, all in one.

We lived in the northwest quarter of town at 208 North Pillsbury Street and I was 10 or 11 that summer. About two alleys north of our house, Pillsbury Street begins its descent toward Little Flat Rock River on the far north end of town. The first hill of the descent, The Big Hill, runs from Mr. Nealy's alley at its crest, crosses West Street, passes one alley on the left, then finishes its run as it flattens out and crosses an open ditch sewer culvert. This shallow ditch was, back in the day, the recipient of all the effluent from the clay tile, backyard septic systems in our section of town. The two-foot-wide open ditch was a small, crystal-clear stream of sweet smelling septic tank run-off most of the year, that reduced itself to a trickle in extra-dry summers. Grandpa's and Grandma's big side yard was just on the other side of the open trench. Then just beyond the ditch and our grandparents' place, North Pillsbury took another dip down toward Little Flat Rock River. Brother Steve and I had explored the ditch pretty thoroughly as kids visiting Grandpa and Grandma. We raced hand-whittled boats, built little stone dams, and trapped shiner minnows as we played on that stream bank in Grandpa's and Grandma's big side yard. Occasionally a sizeable turd would make a surprise appearance down our private stream, so we always wore rubber boots, never bare-footed even on the hottest days.

That summer I had my first stingray bike, a used one my father had brought home from some guy he worked with, some guy whose son had outgrown it – some guy whose son had worn the bike out and had decided that an upgrade was in order was more likely. Though I hadn't yet mastered the wheelie, which I would eventually learn to ride for a full two blocks, I practiced every day. I'm sure I was out practicing wheelies that Saturday when Uncle Jim arrived for a visit and brought our cousin Jimmy with him. Uncle Jim was from Columbus, Indiana, so we only saw cousin Jimmy about once a month in the summers. On this visit, Jimmy, who was two years older than I and one year older than Steve, had brought with him a new Schwinn Stingray Fastback 5-speed – sparkly metallic blue, as I recall, with dual hand brakes, a sleek banana seat, and a stick shift that stuck straight up from the cross bar just in front of that banana seat. I'm sure that rigid chrome stick shift topped with its excruciatingly hard black-plastic handle a little smaller than a pool ball racked many a young boy's balls in its day. It was not the type of feature that could even begin to sneak up on today's safety standards for our coddled, precious children. But this was the mid-sixties, and Ralph Nader was just coming into his prominence, so Uncle Jim and Jimmy got out of the car and pulled the new sparkly blue Schwinn Stingray Fastback 5-speed from the trunk of their family sedan.

"Hey, Uncle Jim!"

"Hey, boys!"

"Nice bike, Jimmy! Looks really fast!"

"It is."

After some ooo-ing and ahhh-ing, Jimmy, Steve, and I mounted our bikes and headed north on Pillsbury Street, intending a trip down The Big Hill to see if Grandpa might be home for a visit.

Now, about halfway down The Big Hill lived a medium-sized, wiry-haired black dog who did nothing but lie on the porch all the live-long day just waiting for boys on bikes. We knew this. This was one mad dog -- not rabid and deranged, mind you, just always angry. When a bike came down The Big Hill, this bulgy-eyed maniac would tear out across his yard snapping and growling as he attempted to grab the leg of any unsuspecting cyclist, pull him from the bike, and proceed to chew on that young man's shin and calf until the owner might come out and pull him off. We knew this. One afternoon we had watched Blackie jerk one of the Miller boys right off his bike and proceed to shred the poor fellow's pant leg, and his left calf to boot. This terminally pissed-off mutt guarded North Pillsbury Street from his porch about 75 feet from the south bank of the open ditch which, you will recall, ran along the base of The Big Hill. Grandpa's house was the next house, about 75 feet from the north bank of the fragrant trickle. About a hundred and fifty feet of open ground lay between the mad dog's lair and Grandpa's front porch, same side of the street.

We also knew, from experience, a few more things: first, that though Blackie was mean and determined, he was just not quite big enough to grab the pant leg of a boy who sped down the hill with his sneakers perched safely on the crossbar of a 20-inch-frame stingray bike, that is as long as that rider had the nerves of steel to steer straight and keep the bike upright; and secondly, we knew that with a stealthy approach and a good head of steam achieved by pedaling like hell down the top half of The Big Hill, by the time a boy was three-quarters the way down the hill and adjacent to Blackie's porch, he had enough reserve to coast the rest of the way down just ahead of the pointy-toothed snapper all the way to the safety of Grandpa's yard, where Blackie would snort, twitch, give up the race, then turn and walk stiff-legged back to his own property to lie in wait.

As we approached the crest of the hill on this particular day, we reminded Jimmy of the menace. Jimmy knew the routine. So, by the time we began our descent, Jimmy had jammed that new blue Stingray Fastback into 5th gear and was already flying down the hill well ahead of my brother and me on our single-speed second-hand jalopies. Sure enough, out came Blackie about the time that we could see Grandpa in the distance sitting in one of those old metal chairs on his front porch. He was watching the challenge unfold. And the pants shredder was so focused on Jimmy and his new stingray bike, that Steve and I easily whizzed right by the menace as he stood sputtering in the middle of North Pillsbury Street, probably admiring that sparkly blue stingray bike that had left him in the dust.

As we pulled up into Grandpa's yard and dismounted, Grandpa eyed Jimmy's new ride.

"Hey, Grandpa!"

"Hey, boys!"

"Thought we'd ride down and show you Jimmy's new bike."

"That's a nice one, Jimmy. How 'bout showing me again how you come down that hill so fast."

"Sure thing, Grandpa."

So, Jimmy, who was no fool, went to the alley just beyond Grandpa's hedge and rode one block west to Pleasant Street. If he turned left on Pleasant then rode one alley, one street, and one more alley back north and made another left he'd complete his safe return over to Pillsbury Street via Mr. Nealy's alley. Like I said, Jimmy was no fool; but even if he were, a fool too would know that even a healthy boy on a brand-new blue 5-speed Stingray Fastback bike can't outrun a mean dog if that boy is pedaling *up* The Big Hill. So as Jimmy was taking the back route to get back to the top of The Big Hill, Grandpa slipped inside before Steve and I knew he has left the porch. In about two minutes, Jimmy appeared at the crest of The Big Hill and we could see him jam that chrome gear shifter into fifth to begin his second impressively speedy descent. Sure enough, at the three-quarter mark, there came the maniacal beast yelping and snapping ferociously at Jimmy. The hell hound was hell-bent on biting a boy that Saturday, and with renewed effort, Blackie seemed to be closing in on Jimmy and his stingray, the shredder a mere three feet behind our cousin, at most. And the bike was beginning to slow because Jimmy was near the flat stretch at the bottom, just about to cross the ditch. And he couldn't put his feet back on the pedals because Blackie could just about snatch that pant leg by then.

Grandpa Richards had been and still was a rabbit hunter. In season, he and Uncle Hubert would take their beagles, Shotgun and Hotrod, hunting and were quite adept at picking off a rabbit running full speed just a few feet from the noses of their hunting dogs that had run some hapless *hasenpfeffer* out of the brush line. Those two marksmen never lost a hunting dog to an errant spray of buckshot, as far as I know.

Just as Steve and I began to feel an itch of concern for cousin Jimmy and the stingray, I heard the front door swing shut behind me and caught a peripheral glimpse of Grandpa as he took one big step down off the side of the porch and about five strides into his side yard, all the while lowering his rabbit gun to his shoulder. Only that time his target was not the pursued, but rather the pursuer; not "the rabbit," but rather the dog. I watched the muzzle of the shotgun steadily track old Blackie for less than two seconds. Then BLAM! Grandpa's shoulder jerked from the buck of the 12-guage blast. Then something almost magical happened. Blackie seemed to slightly levitate for about one half a second then suddenly just disappeared off the other side of North Pillsbury Street. I stepped out onto the road just in time to see the poor son of a bitch skid nose-first down the berm then stop half a foot shy of the sweet stream. Blackie's hind legs kicked stiffly toward the cloudless blue sky two times, then froze in their extended position. Even from my distance I could tell by the mutt's demeanor that his madness had been cured; he didn't look angry anymore… nor surprised at his fate… just dead.

By the time Jimmy and the stingray roll into Grandpa's yard, he was huffing and puffing with eyes big as poker chips and, I suspected, a brown skid mark of his own in his tighty whities that Aunt Louise would deal with when she did the family's laundry on Monday. By the time Jimmy and the stingray arrived, Grandpa had already breached his break-action double barrel, discarded the spent casing, and was entering the house to put the 12-gauge back in the bedroom closet. Then he stepped back out like nothing happened. Nonchalant. Unconcerned.

"That sure is a fast bike, Jimmy."

"Thanks, Grandpa."

And that's all I remember ever being said about the event. Grandpa probably went back inside for a piece of white bread with butter and maple syrup, a cup of coffee, and a nap. And Jimmy, Steve, and I most likely rode those stingrays on down to Little Flat Rock River, at the bottom of the next hill down from Grandpa's on North Pillsbury Street, to see if anyone was fishing.

As I look back, the *incident* of that afternoon, let's call it, had not really seemed that unusual to us at the moment. It all just seemed a little – well – it just seemed a little *Grandpa*. I can't even tell you for sure that we told our dads of "the incident." Furthermore, if Dad or Uncle Jim had much of a response to "the incident" had we told them, I sure don't remember it. They had been raised by Grandpa. There were few surprises left up that old man's sleeve. We all knew his ways, but none of us his rationale, as far as I could ever tell.

Upon hearing this tale, some might view the likes of Grandpa and his ways as a threat to the safety of a small community. As I am remembering Jimmy and that stingray summer, I kind of like to think of Grandpa as our Atticus Finch stepping out onto the main street of Maycomb, Alabama, rifle in hand, ready to save Scout and Jem and Dill and all children from a twitchy rabid dog lumbering down the road toward them. But Blackie certainly was no lumberer when a boy on a bike came down North Pillsbury Street that stingray summer. Besides, I wouldn't read *To Kill a Mockingbird* for another five or six years, and I'd almost bet my lunch money that Grandpa never read it or *any other* novel in his lifetime for that matter. His life had been hard, and I'm guessing that reading skills and rationality had been of limited use to a man growing up through The Great Depression. And maybe Grandpa had just had his fill of that "goddamned son-of-a-bitch shrieking and yelping every time a kid on a bike came rolling down that hill." Had grandpa simply used cousin Jimmy as chum, his own grandson as an unknowing baitfish to lure his un-neighborly annoyance from its front-stoop lair? Like I said, "the incident" never came up in conversation ever again.

Jimmy went home that evening. And whether a witness to "the incident" or not, Grandpa's neighbor, Blackie's keeper as it were, never spoke of it as far as I know. And I think that even a fool wouldn't step across an open ditch to confront a man who had so deftly blasted that fool's pooch as it ran full-tilt-a-snapping at the leg of the fruit-of-the-fruit of the marksman's loins. And even a fool knows that no boy or man can outrun a shotgun blast, uphill *or* down, even on a blue five-speed Schwinn Stingray Fastback. Even a fool's *fool* knows that.

The rest of that summer, as I casually rolled down The Big Hill on my stingray bike, I would, on occasion, peer over into the ditch to check on Blackie's condition. After a week in the summer sun, he had puffed up to twice his size and looked like an industrial version of one of those old-style canister vacuum cleaners: quite cylindrical, but with a good coat of coarse black fur. A few weeks more and Blackie's carcass began to split then cave in on itself, his coarse fur somewhat sparser, though his spindly legs would remain heavenward for another month. By autumn he was mostly skeleton with a small rag of black fur dangling from one of his hind shanks. I stopped and sat astride my stingray and watched it flutter a little on the occasion of an autumn breeze that was passing through one early evening. And just before the first snow, Blackie had been reduced to sun-bleached, stark white bones. Still nose-first down in the ditch and about a half foot from the stream, he reminded me of one of those skeletons we saw sometimes in westerns when some lost prospector or some poor beast had died from desert thirst just steps from a life-saving spring, just over that next hill.

The first snow came and blanketed poor old Blackie, who was far beyond caring at this point, and I think what was left of him must have trickled with the snowmelt into the ditch and washed downstream into Little Flat Rock River. Then Grandpa passed a few years later.

Joy Ride

John Caviness

"Watch out for the telephone poles," hollered Will's best friend from the front seat.

Will barely caught the warning over the "Whoosh. Whoosh. Whoosh." of the telephone poles

The feeling of the hot June air, which was chilled by the marvel of the V8 motor's hard work ran across Will's skin as he leaned out of the car. Sunlight beamed into Will's eyes, he almost couldn't see the telephone poles as the 96' Chevy Impala carried him down that quiet country road he knew all too well. The music on the radio was blasting, *Voodoo* by Godsmack, *"Never did I wanna be here again, and I don't remember why I came..."*

The music faded into the background, as Will glanced behind himself at Sophie, who looked at him in an odd way. She had never gazed at him like this before, normally, when they looked at each other, she would smile, or frown playfully, but this was something else. There was no familiarity in her eyes; her posture sunk into a curl compared to her typical southern belle way of holding herself. The sun was still high in the sky. The wind raged in through the windows of the car, and as he held that car door open, eventually Will realized that she was scared. He took a deep breath, the smell of burnt rubber mixed with summer's familiar scent filled his lungs. He wasn't nervous, for once in his life, yet he still wondered, *How did I get here?*

"Whoosh. Whoosh. Whoosh."

How did I get here? How, indeed . . . .

"Buford! Quit it! That isn't yours!" A few hours earlier, before Trent had started to yell, Will hadn't even noticed that Trent's dog had begun to munch on his last slice of Little Tony's pizza.

"Let him have it." Will said listlessly, "It tastes like cheesy cardboard anyway."

Trent glanced up from his screen briefly, he had been playing a game of *Call of Duty: World at War*, "Dude, you know Buford steals food just so he can punish us later by gassing up the basement."

He reached down quickly after being killed in the game to pet Buford so he knew that his master wasn't seriously angry at him, then chuckled, "I bet Sophie will love that once she gets here, man."

It wasn't the first time Buford caused problems. He was a stumpy-legged mix between a black lab and something else, he was lovable, loyal, but they both knew he was a stupid dog. He would eat anything he could waddle up to regardless of it being food or not.

"Just send him outside, problem solved, man," suggested Will, believing it was the right solution compared to going out in the hot June weather.

Trent paused his game, "Will, why don't we go outside instead? As much as I want to play video games for a while before Sophie eventually takes you into the other room out of boredom since she is oddly attracted to your goofy ass, I would rather go do something today, just to mess up you two's routine. Who knows, it could be fun."

Will thought about it, he figured it could definitely make for a better Saturday afternoon compared to staying inside doing what they had been doing for the past few days. After finishing up the level of the puzzle game he was on, he answered, "I'd hate to make you jealous, why not go outside? Let's skate until she gets here."

Will noticed how Trent's face sort of lit up with jealousy, and Will enjoyed it a bit, maybe too much.

With that, Trent turned off the 360. Though it was a four-year-old refurbished one, it still worked like a dream. Then, without saying a word, the two started cleaning up the place, having accumulated a few days' worth of trash down there, since Will had been staying there for a longer stretches since it was summer vacation. Disgusted looks took hold of their faces as they stacked empty pizza boxes, and groans followed as they gathered gnarly two-liter soda bottles and began stuffing them in the trash bag. Better to clean it now rather than risk the wrath of Trent's mother, who worked long days at the hospital.

Even though Will suggested that they skate, he was an awful skater. Somehow he always managed to lose his balance despite the effort to maintain it. Thankfully, the street where Trent lived was a secluded one, with little traffic. Sometimes there were rocks on it, which didn't help with his inability to skate proficiently, but the give and take of living in the middle of nowhere was a hard thing to compromise. Eventually, they took a break to have some sun tea and when they returned outside with the pitcher and glasses, Sophie showed up. She quickly got out of the car and leaned in the window, reassuring her mom that she'd get a ride home before it got too late.

As she came up the driveway, Trent nudged Will and whispered, "You lucky shit."

Will watched as she slowly sauntered toward them, her sunglasses hugging the bridge of her nose. Her hair was up in a ponytail and she was wearing a tank top, which loosely caressed her torso. Between the branches in the overlying trees her long legs became a spectacle as her skirt danced around her hips with each graceful step. All the while, she accompanied this beautiful appearance with a smile that comes with knowing you have the attention of someone fond. As she drew closer, Will's smile grew wider and wider.

Once she came within a few yards of them, she took off her sunglasses and slowly greeted them, "Hey boys, howsit goin'?"

Neither of them answered at first; as always, they were both a little awestruck by her. Then Trent chuckled, "Good, but we are bored as all get out, good to see ya, Sophie."

As he replied, she walked up to Will, gently put her hands on his shoulders and kissed him, saying, "Good to see you, both. Please tell me we aren't going into that dank cave of a basement on a day like this. " She stepped back and did a flourish with her arms, almost as if she rehearsed the line knowing it would have an effect on the answer.

Will replied as he set the glass of sun tea down, "It would be a shame to watch that smile flip, any ideas as to what we could do?"

She ambled around the driveway playfully, "I was hoping we could go for a drive, Trent, up to driving around a bit?"

Trent took a drink of his tea, checked the time, and then looked back at her, "I'm sure Will here wouldn't mind throwing me some gas money for the time we spend out there, wouldja, Will?"

Will looked away from Sophie briefly and replied, "Yeah man, sounds good to me," then returned to watching Sophie as she threw rocks from the driveway into the street.

"Well, then it is settled, I'll get my keys." Trent hollered as he retreated into the house with a slam of the screen door in the garage.

"You know Will, we could go down by the river for a while later on if you want. Maybe…wait for the sun to go down and the fireflies to come out." Sophie said; knew how to get him to say yes to anything, she would just flash him that look.

It was the sort of look that makes men gamble, the kind of look which gets into a man's soul, and pulls a little bit out with it as she looks away.

"Anything for you," Will answered.

Trent came out of the garage, which snapped Will out of it, and then he commanded, "Alright you two, let's hit the gas station real quick. No one fuck with the radio, if you two are going to be all over each other in the back, I am putting on whatever I want."

The keys jangled as they all silently approached the car, Sophie hanging off Will's arm. Will's head was far in the clouds.

Will sat there and listened to the music. Trent had a large book of CDs in his car, but only ever listened to a fraction of them. By this point, Trent lamented at the current CD, and said that he had heard it too often lately. He quickly ejected and replaced it without taking his eyes off of the road once. He replaced the *System of a Down* album with the first Lamb of God CD, *Ashes of the Wake*. He did this without a care that Sophie was in the car, who was not exactly into music like this. Sophie and Will had no say, since it was Trent's car being used for their joy ride. Trent mouthed the words as the vocalist roared them into the mic, while Will pretended he didn't know every word.

Trent was Will's best friend, a great friend, but he was the worst sort of driver. He consistently sped, always took turns too quickly, and surprisingly never got a ticket despite all this. Nonetheless, the trip to the gas station was brief, though normally it was a longer trip with more cautious drivers. Upon arriving, Will gave him enough cash to last the afternoon for their joy ride. Trent never really minded driving folks around, he enjoyed it, as long as he could choose the tunes and what roads to go down.

The drive seemed to last hours, tons of open road to explore and countryside to see. Occasionally, someone would turn the music down to comment on how beautiful of a day it was, or to dare someone to do something silly. June was often one of the more beautiful and more relentless months. The weather tended to be rather warm and sticky, however, where humans found little comfort, the wildlife and plants were seemingly at their best. Since he was driving, and no one trusted his judgment in daring, Trent was immune to the dares, so it was more of a show for him than that of a game.

Will and Sophie went back and forth, first making each other do innocent or silly things. Will dared Sophie to sing off-key since she was in choir. Sophie dared Will to take his socks off and hold them out of the window, which given the wind was risky business. Then Sophie upped the ante, and Will would raise it, keeping the fire of the game alive. Eventually Will dared Sophie to take her top off and lean out of the window, which she shamelessly did, since no one was around but Trent and Will. Sophie came back at him and dared Will to climb from the back seat to the front seat through the side windows. He only did it because he knew it was a tired old trick; he'd done it many times with no dare involved. Their game upped the tension between them, and Sophie loved it. Will, however, was getting tired of it.

After a while, they listened to the music in the background as they sat close to one another, smiling like young lovers do on a summer afternoon. After a short break from daring had elapsed, Trent looked into the rearview and made eye contact with Will, "Wanna do something crazy?"

Will smiled and said nothing. Sophie saw this as an opportunity. She looked down at her legs, then out the window. Her hair was down now, flowing in the wind as Trent went as quickly as he wanted down those old country roads.

"I want you to jump." she half whispered to Will; she was still looking out the window.

Will thought that she was fucking with him, "Trent, turn the radio down. Say what?"

This wasn't like her, he thought to himself. She put her hands on her knees, inhaled the wind blowing over her, then turned and looked at Will.

There was that look again, followed by, "I want you to jump. I want you to jump out of the car. I dare you to jump, as proof."

Will gazed into the seat in front of him after she dared, stunned.
Trent looked back at them, in the mirror, and asked, "Proof of what?"

"Proof that I mean something to him. What do you say, Will? Prove yourself to me."

This wasn't like her, he thought again. It wasn't so much how she asked him to do it, as it was that she seemed driven to ask him to do it. Will looked at her; he wasn't sure if it was really happening or not, but he remained silent as he thought of what to do at this crossroad. The song *Morningstar* played in the background, in a language only two of the people in the car understood.

"I double-dog dare you, Will. And if you don't do it, there goes your honor and your girl."

Trent knew what his words would mean; he brought Will's honor into question. Trent knew that Will wasn't brave. Will was quiet, unless he had to be loud. He was kind, unless he had to be mean. He was a coward, unless he had to be brave. Will considered the facts, throwing honor in the backseat and focused on Sophie. He wondered what she would think if he didn't do it. She hadn't said a word, she hadn't even looked at him after asking him. She distanced herself from him as well, and seemed to be waiting for his response.

After what seemed like an eternal silence, filled only by the sound of the motor running and the telephone poles whooshing as the car flew by them, Will looked down at his feet, and broke the silence with, "Go out by East 206th, I'll do it."

Trent stopped, turned the car around, blared the song *Stone by Stone*, and set on towards that part of the sticks.

Sophie didn't say a thing as they drew nearer and nearer to the fields out by East 206th street.

Will hollered at Trent, "Do me a favor. Don't slow down for nothin'. If you do, I won't know when to jump. If you do, you'll be explaining this shit to people for a long time, man." He paused, then said, "You were right about going outside today, this has been a damn good Saturday."

Sophie still didn't say a word to Will, but for the first time all day, she was wearing her seatbelt.

The telephone poles stood guard in front of the fields, as if they were mocking Will. He looked at the door, and the window. First, he rolled the window up and unbuckled his seat belt. He had gone down this road a thousand times, but he had never felt like this while doing so. Will held the door open against the wind with one arm, with the other holding him steady on the frame of the car.

How did I get here?

"Watch out for the telephone poles," hollered Will's best friend from the front seat.

Will barely caught the warning over the sound of the telephone poles, "Whoosh. Whoosh. Whoosh."

The feeling of the hot June air, which was chilled by the marvel of the V8 motor's hard work, ran across Will's skin as he leaned out of the car. Sunlight beamed into Will's eyes, he almost couldn't see the telephone poles as the 96' Chevy Impala carried him down that quiet country road he knew all too well. The music on the radio was blasting, *Voodoo* by Godsmack, *"Never did I wanna be here again, and I don't remember why I came..."* The music faded into the background, as Will glanced behind himself at Sophie, who looked at him in an odd way.

It isn't how one measures a jump, but rather how one times it. Where it takes place, why it becomes a binding commitment, who jumps and who sees the jump, all factor into the timing. The long, two-way country road fell between two fields. On the right hand field, the only thing growing was patchy thin grass, which bordered a large barn used for storing hay and tractors. On the left hand side of the road, there were corn fields as far as the eye could see. A wide parallel array of wire held up by tall, thick wooden poles spanned for miles along the road in both fields.

Things weren't always great between Sophie and Will. Most of the time, actually, they fought, argued, and then made up soon thereafter, but they both were fond of each other enough to come back to one another. Perhaps they were simply too fond, too young, perhaps even both simultaneously in addition too stubborn to listen to anyone outside of each other. People would always ask Will how he landed a beautiful girl like Sophie, and he never knew what to say to them. Often after not receiving a good answer, they would bring up how often the two fought with one another and argued with each other, and how the fighting lasted longer than the peacetimes. His closer friends would tell him it wasn't worthwhile being with her due to that; the others told him never let go.

On some level, he knew that he loved that girl. All he ever wanted to do was make her smile, despite how bad things at home were, or how rough the times were for her. He knew he wasn't the best at it, but he always tried. He'd broken rules for her, without a single doubt in his mind it was worth it. Will often thought to himself, *Will and Sophie. That is simply how it should be.* He didn't mind putting himself at risk for her, not this time or any other time. Gambling valuable, abstract things like his well-being didn't matter to him as long as it brought that smile back. This time she had asked him to prove it to her, again.

He chose this road for a reason; it was the main road she would take into town, probably for years to come. As he looked back to her, while syncing his breathing to the sound of the telephone poles whooshing by, he smiled at her, hoping to pull that look of hers out that he loved so much. The attempt resulted in nothing. The wind raged in through the windows of the car, and as he held that car door open, Will realized that Sophie was scared. He took a deep breath, the smell of burnt rubber mixed with summer's familiar scent filled his lungs.

He wasn't nervous, for once in his life, yet he still silently wondered, *How did I get here?* As he asked himself this, he released his right arm from the chassis of the car. His mind cleared as his feet left the edge of the car, loosening his left hand's grip on the door just as his torso cleared door's the swing radius. Then he heard the door slam behind him as he went through the air, almost as if he were suspended in time. Before Will reached the protective line of telephone poles, he looked up into the clouds, and closed his eyes.

"Whoosh. Thump. Whoosh."

Trent heard the thump and slammed on the brakes, which sent a screech through the humid air in the two surrounding fields. He got out and couldn't see Will.

All Trent could hear was Sophie's sobbing. "Why did you make me do that?!"

Her cries faded as he ran towards approximately where Will landed.

As Trent reached Will, Will opened his eyes, looked up at Trent, and whispered, "Well, this definitely isn't Heaven."

Trent looked down at him, smiled, and asked, "So how was it, you alright?"

Will extended his hand, Trent grabbed it and helped him up, and replied, "My side hurts a little bit from the landing, but I'm alright."

As they ambled toward the car, Trent threw his arm over Will's shoulder.

"She's pretty shook up by all this, y'oughtta talk a while once she calms down. I'll drop you by the river."

Will hopped into the car, winced as he landed in the seat and expected Sophie to be happy he was okay, which never came to pass. He at least expected her to say something, but instead all he heard was her softly sobbing while the lyric, "*Never did I wanna be here again, and I don't remember why I came...*" brought the song to a close.

Trent pulled up to the backside of the covered bridge, which was near the riverbed, and as the couple climbed out, he hollered out of the window, "See you back at my place!"

The river was always quiet, with a slow-moving current. Today the water seemed as though it wasn't flowing at all. There was no one there, not that there ever really were many people there since the pollution scandal which hit the papers a few years previously scared them all away. Sophie calmed down while they looked for a grassy patch near the water and once they found it, they had a seat.

"I'm glad you are okay; I want you to know that. I can't believe you did that. You jumped for me," she whispered between sniffles.

"Of course I jumped for you. I'd do it again, and make Trent drive faster if you asked me to prove myself again."

"I never should have listened to his stupid idea."

Will was confused. "What? Wait. What do you mean, 'his idea'? *You* asked me to do it."

Sophie sighed and answered, "It was his idea to make you jump. He figured you wouldn't do it. That way you wouldn't have to find out..." She looked away as her words trailed off.

Will felt fury, and a hollowing loss, burrowing inside, but he stayed calm.

"Find out what?"

She scooted away from him, grabbed some pebbles and threw them in the river, making a grapeshot ripple effect on the still water.

"He figured you wouldn't do it, and then I could break up with you cleanly, without having to tell you that he and I have been sleeping together behind your back. I'm sorry."

There is a torment that comes with betrayal. It robs a person of their current understanding of their surroundings, their place in the world. Will's eyes opened as wide as they could, but he could no longer see. His pupils raced from side to side as he tried to wrap his head around what he just heard. He gazed out at the polluted river, then stood up, staggering for balance, and looked down at her.

"I jumped for you."

Keeping Still
DeMaris Gaunt

Perfect World

John Gilmore
(song lyric)

Sat down to think but my thoughts they all scattered
I could gather 'em back but what would it matter
I mean maybe I could, but why even try
took a drink of my coffee, leaned back and closed my eyes

Then I looked up as my darlin' walked in
She gave me a kiss and asked how I'd been
I said, "much better now my beautiful friend"
That made her smile so she kissed me . . . again

We took a walk in the garden and I picked her some flowers
then we laid around the house for a couple of hours
couldn't imagine a place in the world any better
wished I could stay right there with her . . . forever

So that's just the that my morning went by
well, no . . .
   really . . . . It's not and when I opened my eyes
   my coffee was cold and the morning had flown
   away in a daydream

There goes my mind off wandering again
it always comes back. I just never know when
So, here I sit and here I'll stay
While a part of me is worlds away
Worlds away from reality
Oh the places I go and the things that I see
But I'd never come back . . . no, I'd never come back . . .
If it was up to me

There's the things that I have
but a lot more that I want
some dreams come true but most of mine don't
So I warmed up my coffee and thought, "What do I care"
I yawned and I stretched and sat right back down in my chair

There goes my mind off wandering again
it always comes back. I just never know when
So, here I sit and here I'll stay
While a part of me is worlds away
Worlds away from reality
Oh the places I go and the things that I see
But I'd never come back . . . no, I'd never come back . . .
If it was up to me

Milk Bath
Annie Oberman

I know a man
Janet Moore

I know a man who grew up in Chicago. The neighborhood was very depressed. His father he did not see much, and the times that he did, they were not pleasant.

I know a man whose mother had an abusive boyfriend. Violence, drugs, violence floating in and out. Anger and fear in daily doses. This anger and fear leached out in his life.

The World around him seemed hopeless. But something in his heart said, "This World around me, does not define me."

I know a man who began to write his thoughts on paper. He rapped them out to his friends. Passion and ambition were born. The first glimmer of light. It felt so good. He was defining himself. No matter what happened around him now -

Now he found a way to ground himself. He did not listen to critics, slashers of dreams.

I know a man, at the age of 16 with lots of guts and his buddies, to NYC did they drive.

Barely limping there. He thought, "once they hear us, we will have a record deal!"

They received closed doors, judgmental eyes, and discouraging words.

That same feeling at home returned, that pain in the gut over and over. He began to think thoughts of self destruction.

I know a man who looked at his words and decided that he could feel good about himself no matter what anyone said. He learned that anger and fear met disbelief in his heart.

I know a man who began to learn the art of action. He looked at his options. Realistically, what can be done to remove oneself of horrible surroundings? He decided to take action with his education.

To the high school counselor he marched, with his new enthusiasm.

I know a man, in his senior year, who asked, "What do I need to do to get my grades on track to go to college". He was met with eyes just short of laughter, and told he would have to go three more years to acquire enough credits. Again that pit in his gut formed that familiar reaction. Hopelessness.

I know a man who remembered his words and felt his ambition get stronger. He will make another decision, a decision of action. The more he gave his ambition energy, the stronger it got. He decided to quit, and get his GED. I know a man who started looking for a job. It seemed the only source of income involved theft or drugs. But, he pressed on. He found a job at a flower shop, delivering flowers. He received constant ridicule and laughter at his choice. But, anger had turned into determination. With his job, he would pay for his GED and go to college. His new freedom of choice and a paycheck cultivated his confidence.

With his first check he started looking for his first place. The next choice was to change his environment. Well, the neighborhood didn't change, his nucleus did.

I know a man who was having a hard time in his new world of responsibility. This man lit candles. The glow was soft and cozy in his apartment. His lady friends enjoyed it. Little did they know that the electric had been turned off. This lesson of choice of attitude was powerful. He figured out if he got a 25-cent-per-hour raise, that would be enough money to pay for his GED class. When he shared this news with his boss, the boss's response was, "This is not a career, it's a job – I'm not giving you the raise." That familiar sinking feeling returned, but it had a shorter life. He returned to his words. The rhymes ignited him. Strength grew and grew. Time and effort was the next lesson learned.

I know a man that studied on his own and passed his GED. "Now," he said, "I want to teach. I am going to college!" His decision was Purdue University. Then he learned that the entrance requirements alone closed the door in his face, let alone the cost. It was devastating. But...his mind was learning to think another way. Persistency was getting stronger.

I know a man that allowed his will to change. He decided that if he could not attend the school, he still wanted to be in it. With this determination, he got a job as a janitor at the university. With this choice, he removed himself from his familiar neighborhood and stepped a foot closer to his dream. Wow, for the first time he was around people who thought differently. This shift brought on a whole new set of words and fire. The power of creative expression! Battling his words in the moment as they flowed. He felt lifted. His enthusiasm flowed over to all that heard him or were around him. At the school, he did his job with gusto. People couldn't help but love his outlook and charm. He was contagious. One day, he shared his dream with the staff at the school. Now finally, here were people who did not laugh. They understood options, choice, and dedication. They were rooting for him. Do you know how good but strange this felt for him? They made him wise in the ways of employee benefits and financial aid. And, because he was working so hard and his passion was overflowing, his newfound admirers were determined to do whatever it took to get him in the school.

I know a man that couldn't wait to be in class now. His grades reflected this. More and more people he met of the same mind. Rap battling, good grade gettin', college student, mind sponge, positive, working dude! People just wanted to be near him, because he walked in his truth. The power of choice and action, sometimes slow - always rewarded accordingly. He declared he must be a teacher. He will make a difference in children's lives. He was crazed in both his learning and creating. In the end of this chapter, he had a diploma in one hand and Rap-battling trophies in the other. Well-wishes sent him off to his life as a teacher and a husband. This woman in his life showed him strength he had not seen before. It was so refreshing.

I know a man that moved himself to yet another environment. He saw a new tolerance of culture. Culture intermingling. Living beside each other, and he saw it in Indianapolis. This inspired him. His words have a message.

I know a man that became an elementary school teacher. Once he was living his dream, he decided…he couldn't stand it. "I am trained" he proclaimed, "but I can't do this!" Even though this was stunning to him, he realized that this dream brought him to this point. Not everything unfolds how we expect it. It is bigger and better. Beyond comprehension at the time.

I know a man that believed in himself. He went to that place within and continued his focus on his writing rapping world. He stopped teaching elementary school and started working with wayward teens. They gravitated toward him and hung on his words. They challenged him and he challenged them. Bless this man, blessed with words, compassion, and energy.

I know a man that is in action. So much now, he had a double life. Both worlds pulled at him.

Remember, it's choice and action. He had an incredible flow on. His insatiable passion with his words could not be stopped. He began to realize that his undying passion was to bring messages to the world. The birthright of his birth name carries the energy of a revolutionary. This was awakening more and more every day.

I know a man, that while all this growth is going on, personal drama was tearing away at him. He goes to the safest place he knows. That place within. That connection that brings the words. It brings logic. It brings choice. It brings action. It dissolves anger and fear. The music world called to him so much, he stopped teaching the teens and started teaching the world. I give thanks for those who teach by example. They move through roadblocks and disapproval.

I know a man that has this message for the world. His light shines so brightly in all the darkness. I give thanks for his vibration and inspiration. All of the intentions in the music world are not the same as his, but, he knows how to move around in it. He sees so much that is not right. But, he is patient, for he knows about timing and the finesse of charm. He has learned by living in persistency and being a shapeshifter. He doesn't give up.

I know a man that just won a Grammy. I am proud of him and look forward to all the gifts he brings to the world.

Remember, your world is what you believe, believe in yourself.

Heavyhearted
Annie Oberman

Mark Twain and The Saddest Boy in the World
Radka Caviness

It is autumn 1947 in Portland, Oregon. I am eight years old and have recently started the fourth grade at Beach Grade School, our new school. Before we moved, my older sister Olga and I attended Abernathy – we are both happier at Beach.

Classmates live nearby. Closest is Douglas. He lives across the alley from me. I can look across the narrow unpaved alley and see Douglas (9) and his brother David (7) playing. I watch their father play catch with them and see their pretty mother always smiling at them. My friend Loretta lives at the west end of the alley and my friend Joan across the street at the end of our long block. Another friend, Chester (9), lives a block east of me with his two older brothers and his younger brother Leroy (7). They are orphans and live with their grandparents.

Chester and Leroy are inseparable, always playing with Douglas and David. Chester and Douglas are best friends and Leroy and David are best friends. I always know after school I will see the four of them in the backyard across the alley.

At school, Mrs. Hollingsworth, our teacher reads *The Adventures of Tom Sawyer and Huckleberry Finn* to us at the end of each day. We all think this book is wonderful; we clear our desks and listen, enraptured.

One day, I see Douglas and David's father finding scrap wood, nails, and a hammer for them. Then each afternoon I watch Douglas, Chester, David, and Leroy building. Douglas and Chester take turns with the hammer and David and Leroy hand nails to them. Douglas and David's mother brings them cookies and Kool-Aid on a tray and smiles happily at them, admiring their wood-working.

When Douglas and David's father comes home each evening, they show him their day's work and he also smiles as they go in to dinner.
One day, Douglas, Chester, Leroy, David, and I are walking home from school. They are ahead of me and walking fast. They go straight to Douglas and David's house. Usually, Chester and Leroy go home first and then go to Douglas and David's.

I go home, change my clothes, and run out to play. I see no one is in

Douglas' yard. A short time later his mother comes out and calls them. She waits a few minutes and then goes to the corner and looks towards Chester and Leroy's house. She calls again and then crosses the street and walks east. She returns with Chester and Leroy's grandmother. They are alarmed and perplexed.

Unknown to any of us, Douglas, David, Leroy, and Chester have taken their handiwork around the corner and down Going Street straight west – less than a mile to Swan Island; to the Willamette River.

Four small boys proudly carrying their small wooden platform.

My father works at Swan Island. He's one of the lucky few who remain of the tens of thousands who worked one of three shifts building ocean-going supply ships, the Liberty Ships for the Second World War. Now Merchant Marine Ships dock at Swan Island for repairs and refurbishing. There is no shore – only the deep channel of the Willamette River going north to join the Columbia River and then the Pacific Ocean.

The four boys launch their raft into the deep, cold, swift river; it overturns; Chester somehow manages to hang on. Chester Rollins is seen clinging to the raft and is rescued – only Chester.

Immediately everyone says it is a miracle Chester survived; but very soon everyone blames him. I don't understand why adults are blaming him. Mrs. Hollingsworth read us *The Adventures of Tom Sawyer and Huckleberry Finn*. Mark Twain is to blame. On a sunny Oregon afternoon Douglas, David, Leroy – and Chester, too – were forever lost. I believe that, for fortune and fame, Mark Twain has sent other boys to their doom.

I know I will never read Mark Twain.

In the fifth and sixth grades, Chester comes over and shoots marbles with me. He knows I love marbles and he always lets me win one of his marbles.

I know why he really comes. As we play, he looks into Douglas and David's backyard. I know what he sees.

Chester looks until he can't look anymore – then he picks up his marbles and goes home.

(How) To Kill a Mockingbird or Two Men and a Truck

Steve VandeWater
(song lyric)
Honorable Mention, Song Lyric/Poetry Category

Roane County's road crew was out on the job,
Two old men name of Billy and Bob.
They'd both retired from other careers,
And both were getting up there in years.

As volunteers, they worked for free
To help their small community.
Never expecting any pay,
They did it just to fill their day.

Their job was easy; not much to it
But no one else wanted to do it;
Drive around in a county truck,
Find roadkill, and pick it up.

Not many men would have the will
Or stomachs strong as Bob and Bill
But even though the job was gross,
Bill and Bob were not like most.

"They're a little off" became the rumor
When folks discussed their sense of humor.
For though upon a ghastly run,
The guys were always having fun.

For instance, once they found a skunk
And hid it in the Sheriff's trunk.
And once Jeanette, an office girl
Opened her drawer to a flattened squirrel.

Despite their victims' loud objection
The county relied upon carcass collection
So the boss dared only to slap their wrist,
Warning "Next time, you'll be dismissed!"

One day within the month of June
They came upon a dead raccoon.
Rigor mortis had set about,
So its legs were stiff and stuck straight out.

Bill got out, and in joyful bliss,
Hollered to Bob, "Hey! Look at this!"
He tipped the cadaver back up on its feet
And it stood there like that, on the side of the street.

"You know, driving by going 45,
you'd swear that that thing is still alive!
I wonder what folks passing by might do,
If it stood right here for a day or two."

So they left it like that, and drove away,
Checking back the following day.
Still standing there, but starting to reek,
It didn't fall down until later that week.

By the time Bernice down at City Hall
Told the guys she'd had some calls,
Bob and Bill had secretly planned
A prank so outrageous, they'd surely get canned.

Now the problem with roadkill is that it gets germy,
So the guys studied mail order taxidermy
To preserve all the animals sure to be found
As they drove down the county roads, making their rounds.

Their collection soon grew to be quite a menagerie
Of critters whose lives ended sudden and tragically.
There were foxes and squirrels and possums and rabbits
Small animals cursed with poor road-crossing habits.

However, they also picked up a few deer
To add to the group by the end of the year.
Tirelessly working to get them all mounted,
When finished, near 45 specimens counted.

For amateurs, Bill and Bob showed great skill
You'd never have guessed that these things were roadkill.

Appearing as lifelike as you'd ever see
To folks speeding down County Road 23.

The guys had determined to make their big play
On a cold and blustery December day
So at 3 am, loaded trailer in tow,
The guys headed out in the flurrying snow.

At 6:45 in their usual haunt,
Marjorie's Family Restaurant,
The guys sipped their coffee and watched morning news
A late-breaking story on Channel 2

Now Marjorie's always drew a big crowd
The atmosphere cramped, and awfully loud
But today you could almost have heard a pin drop
As the crowd watched the news in the old coffee shop.

The news feature showed County Road 23
And Marjorie's patrons could clearly see
A bright yellow Animal Crossing sign
And a bunch of wild animals standing in line.

They stretched cross the road, lined up tail to snout
Cars were stopped, the drivers too scared to get out.
Afraid of being mauled or trampled, or bitten.
The newslady stood in her long coat and mittens.

She asked a bystander a boatload of questions,
A toothless old yokel, who gave his suggestions.
She asked "What would cause them to act in this way?"
He said "Maybe rabies! Or God's Judgement Day!"

The crowd back at Marjorie's Restaurant roared,
"It's Scooter! That crazy old man's off his gourd!"
"Is it some kind of unwritten rule that they choose
The stupidest people for their interviews?"

The coverage kept up 'til the police got there.
Sergeant Ray fired several shots in the air
He thought that the varmints would scatter and run
But apparently they weren't afraid of his gun.

So he cautiously walked up and nudged with his toe
A groundhog that fell on its face in the snow.
Ray stood there all puzzled and scratching his head
These beasts were not simply immobile, but DEAD!

Now who in the world would get their weird kicks,
By causing a traffic jam out in the sticks?
What kind of a person had that kind of brain?
Were they just bored or completely insane?

Proceeding to knock all the animals down,
The cops cleared the road leading back into town.
The anchor reported the whole thing a hoax
"Prob'ly just kids playing practical jokes."

The coffee shop's elderly waitress named Mable
Slyly winked at the two as she wiped off their table.
She'd guessed at their guilt by the looks in their eyes
She tore up their bill as she said, "Nice one, guys!"

So they both gave her large and generous tips
As they walked from the joint with big smiles on their lips.
Bob chuckled at Bill, and Bill grinned at Bob
What a great way to start a new day on the job!

Sometimes
Kid Quill

Sometimes I'm loved
Sometimes I'm alone

Sometimes I feel lost
Sometimes I feel home

Sometimes I feel happy
and sometimes I laugh

But sometimes sad
when I think of the past

Sometimes I'm scared
and sometimes I fail

Sometimes I'm brave
and sometimes I prevail

Sometimes I'm busy
Sometimes I'm lazy

Sometimes I'm sane
Sometimes I'm crazy

But sometimes I'm human
and sometimes I love

That I'm sometimes worried
by all the above.

Kid Quill (photo by Sally Meyer)

Indiana's Lyrical Underdog

Sally Meyer

Mitch pulled his Depauw soccer hat over his head as a light November drizzle started to come down. We were waiting outside the Uptown Cafe, vying with the church-goers for the next available table to open up, as two hungover millennials typically do on a Sunday morning. We talk cynically about mega-churches and he brings up some charity work he did with his grandma at her church that week.

"I'm lucky I didn't catch on fire when I stepped inside," he jokes.

When we're finally seated, he catches sight of a man across the room who's indulging in a heaping plate of something worth envying.

"I have to go ask him what he ordered," Mitch says before he makes his way over to the gentlemen and taps him on the shoulder.

One main thought was going through my mind as I listened over the buzz of the crowded diner.

"Excuse me, sir, sorry to bother you, but your meal looks so good. I was wondering what you ordered," I hear him say.

The guy answers casually and Mitch returns to our table, seeming pleased with life as usual, his signature dimple pressed into his cheek. I couldn't help but feel a sense of irony because the guy he approached has no idea who Mitch is, and most people don't. Though Mitch was born and raised in Indiana, no one in the jam-packed diner recognized him as the twenty-three year old recording artist known as Kid Quill.

When I tried to decide what angle to come at this from, I realized most people reading this would be hearing the name Kid Quill for the first time. When you learn that a guy from Shelbyville, Indiana has had not one, but two albums achieve top ten status on the iTunes hip hop/rap charts, most readers would probably have the same reaction as I did. Disbelief. Much of the music that skyrocketed his last two albums to such a status were written in between classes at Depauw, and recorded at a private studio in Noblesville. The first show I ever saw of his, I was just there by happenstance; his buddy Nick had arranged for him to play at a fraternity in Terre Haute. That night in September, Nick passed me in one of the hallways and he was full of energy.

"Dude his album just reached top ten on iTunes *today*," Nick informed me.

I was immediately skeptical. If this guy were all that good, I would have already heard about him. I was so wrong.

Mitch is no stranger to the notion that his success sometimes seems fictional. And neither are his fans. His claim as one of the most underrated artists in the industry might come across as self-inflated if it not for the constant echo from his fanbase. His twitter is cluttered with mentions by listeners from Luxembourg to Greece, all screaming that Kid Quill is "still underrated." I wondered why this might be the case and speculate it may be due in part to the fact that Mitch makes tracks that are best consumed the way people used to listen to music. My dad once described to me how he and his friends would go buy a new record and sit in someone's living room and listen to it from start to finish. And that was a Friday night for them back then.

There was something I loved so much about this notion, and it's an idea I keep returning to when I think of how best to describe Mitch's music. It's perhaps why he is so cynical of the radio. He's not really in the business of pumping out singles that just sound like clickbait looks. It's true what they say, that if you make something with too much mass appeal it's usually garbage. Since we met I've been telling him that his music is for people with attention spans, a notion especially important to a fan base like his. It should be a comforting concept for the potential of the what's to come when we consider that it's targeted towards the most educated generation thus far. His growing listener base consumed over fifteen million minutes of Kid Quill tracks on Spotify in 2017 alone. It could be argued that these people want relief from artists who are just having deep thoughts about shallow things. And in that way, Mitch does have his finger on the pulse of a generation. The positivity he preaches ties people to his music at a time when the influx of information makes negativity in our world so hard to run from. He's really the opposite of dark and even when his lyrics are rooted in something heavy, there's a redeeming quality to it, one that's not there by accident. He's just as positive and introspective as his sound is.

"I was so happy that people liked my music, because in a way it was like they were accepting me," he explains.

But unfortunately, that hasn't been enough.

To his fans, he may seem larger than life, but in reality, when an order is placed for Kid Quill merchandise, it is Mitch himself in his parents' basement who boxes it up, sends it out, and then returns to his notebook, waiting to be noticed by the right people. If you type in Kid Quill on Google, one of the top popular searches is "net worth," but it yields no real results. This is due to the fact that so far there are none to be had, besides the simple fourteen karat yellow gold chain that never leaves his wrist. You won't see him without it on, which isn't surprising given what it means to him.

"It was the first thing I bought when I started making money," he tells me.

Besides purchasing studio time, it might be one of the only things he's really managed to buy, a testament to the massive amount of student loan debt he and most others in his generation carry. It makes you wonder how a person could be as successful and frugal as Mitch and still live at their parents' house and stress about student loan debt.

It's clear he's walking a fine line and I can easily imagine why. Struggling to become famous is weird for someone who doesn't like to brag. He's incredibly smart and doesn't feel the need to let people know it, graduating 8th in his class at Shelbyville. Every song is sprinkled with Easter eggs you might not pick up on unless you're paying attention. He does a good job of composing lyrics with multiple meanings, so what you get out of his music might be different than the person sitting next to you. His song "Soapbox" is perhaps my favorite example of this, mainly because it's clear the election of Donald Trump has called to the forefront voices of many who usually prefer to avoid ruffling feathers, Mitch among them. Undoubtedly humble, he goes to the gym all the time, but thinks "being jacked would be weird," he tells me. But it wasn't until he explained to me how he had randomly met a rapper easily a thousand times more famous than he is, that I realized Mitch can't stand to be even a little pretentious. At a friend's apartment in downtown Indy, he pulled out his phone and shows me the photo taken that day of he and the artist at some fast food joint.

"Oh my god, did you tell him who you are?!" I asked excitedly.

"Nah," he says, shoving his phone back in his pocket and peering around the room, ready for a change in conversation.

Though the rapper in the photo with him has had countless singles and achievements, and his biography on YouTube measures him worth about 4.5 million, he has never had two albums hit top ten status on iTunes. *But Mitch has.*

Fast forward and the rainy November day has been replaced by a snowy December one. Our stomachs are grumbling but our bank accounts aren't exactly full either so we forego brunch. It's another Sunday morning. This time off a side street in Broad Ripple. We were sitting in the car for longer than people usually do because this kind of company is hard to come by and today goodbyes are postponable.

He plays me a new song he's working on called "Weatherman" and amid the chills it gives me I fail to immediately recognize the irony of the title as the snow comes down.

With Mitch you forget you're talking to a rapper and the side of him that is a political science minor and interpersonal communications major starts to show. He's a comforting endless conversation type of person. But eventually silence falls and he sort of becomes someone else for a minute.

"Do you think you'll always live in Indy?" he asks me, staring out the window as the first snowfall of the season starts to stick.

You can see in his face that winter weighs more heavily on him than it does on most. I tell him I'm not sure yet, but I wanna come back and have kids here someday, maybe like how sea turtles return to where they were born. He laughs, that dimple again appearing in his cheek before he makes his point.

"I wanna be the guy from Indy," he says.

He references several artists and the places they're from, explaining that there's no one from Indy yet, and he wonders why shouldn't it be him after all. I can't help but agree. He loves this place so much. What a sincere soul he's got. I wondered how many more seasons he would spend as the unknown underdog walking among the crowd.

Filter
DeMaris Gaunt

The filter is on
and love is squirming
twisting
trying to say
what it feels
like it needs to say
but I am the gatekeeper
who decides
how much
should be revealed
and I have one finger
on the trigger
one foot on the gas
another finger
over the barrel
and one heel
about to catch fire
from all this friction
all this dragging
all this restraint
that is supposed
to save me
from embarrassment
and the sudden
doe-eyed expression
on my face
that contains
every truth I can
never say.

THINK
John Caviness

Photographer's Note: This sign hangs in the common area of the CICS graduate student offices, where we are challenged to battle our assignments and professors with our wits.

Quadratic Equation
DeMaris Gaunt

Lonely
isn't
being alone
on a cold
November evening
watching the trees
release their orange
confetti
into the wind
and lonely
has nothing to do
with silence
or the dark shadows
that slowly
enter your room
and lonely
isn't
in the open space
between the stars —
lonely
is the
navigable road
between two houses
it's the closable
distance
that goes unclosed
lonely
is your otherwise
empty hand
holding
a photograph
of someone
you love
who loved you

not enough
to feel the absence
of your face
as a problem
that needed to be
examined
and solved.

The Purple Fairy (CAPTURED!)
Alys Caviness-Gober

The Purple Fairy Train

Alys Caviness-Gober

Once upon a time in Noblesville, back when you could hear train whistles blow and conductors call out, *Aaaaallllllllll aaaa-booooard!*, you'd see trains go through town, you could wave at conductors and passengers and they'd all wave back with big happy smiles on their faces! Did you know fairies always rode our town's trains back then? They sure did!

Fairies can be invisible to the human eye and they're pretty good at hiding. In fact they look a lot like butterflies, so even when you squint to try to see 'em when you ride a train, you might miss 'em. But, they're there, because fairies *LOVE* trains! Their wings get tired of flapping; train rides are their favorite other way to travel! And, did you know that every fairy has his or her own train, and that they live in red cabooses, and that fairy trains go on right the same tracks as our trains? Isn't that cool?!? And, just like fairies, the fairy trains can be invisible, so when you see a fairy train, well, it's like seeing a rainbow or a four-leaf clover! It makes the whole day special!

My favorite fairy train has always been *The Purple Fairy Train*, because purple's my favorite color! I'd squint and squint and see it now and then, whisking by as the wind sang through our town's leafy trees. What color Fairy Train did *YOU* ever see go by on our town's train tracks? I bet you saw *ALL* of them!

Now, the fairies here have been sad for a while, because a handful of mean old greedy wizards stopped our town's trains from running. And now those mean old greedy wizards are trying to tear out all the tracks so no trains can ever run again! That made all the fairies so sad. Some of them packed up their fairy trains and left. My favorite fairy train, *The Purple Fairy Train*, left. I heard it's off running on some other town's train tracks, where the wind sings through *their* leafy trees. I squint, but, just like all trains in our town, I don't see it anymore.

Maybe if that handful of mean old greedy wizards leave the train tracks alone, *The Purple Fairy Train* will come back to our town when our trains start running again.

I sure hope so – *don't YOU?*

A Week in the Life of . . .

Jo Mader
Third Place, Song Lyric/Poetry Category

Tuesday, late afternoon

My bare, ringed hand
slapped the plate-glass,
thuds and clicks
to those on the other side.

Some ignored it,
others looked up, puzzled
then away,
'til one woman,
seeing my wide eyes
and blue-tinged skin
waved and pointed.

I slapped faster,
harder,
adding car keys to my noise makers.
No voice –
my breathing loud,
harsh,
a freight train going nowhere.

The guard came to me
through a magical hole
in the glass.
"Star Trek," I thought,
He shouted odd words
over my head –
Code! STAT!!

Women came from everywhere,
coats the colors of Easter eggs.

A man in white asked questions
I had no breath to answer.
They cut off my dress
and bra.
I went to sleep
propped against a Gurney cart.

Friday evening

"Climbed ten flights of stairs,"
I told her.
"No, Mom, not ten flights – ten
steps."
"Right," I said. "No door."
"The door was there. You couldn't
find it.
 Oxygen deprivation, Mom."
"Right," I said.
"Talk to Dad. I want to sleep."
She did and I did.

Sunday morning

My roommate is tethered
to a plastic tube
long enough
to let her wander
from her bed
by the window,

passed my bed
into the bathroom, or
even more exciting,
two feet into the hallway.
She can see
the nurses station,
watch elevator doors
open and close,
nod to neighbors' visitors,
and flag down Candy Stripers
pushing carts with
books, papers
and magazines.

She can't go far.
She can't go fast.
She can't get a kink
in her oxygen line,
but, she can go farther
than I can and I'm jealous.

Monday morning

I want a shower.
I haven't had a shower
since last Tuesday morning.
Patients on 8West are only
permitted sponge baths.
Patients on 8West typically
die within 72 hours of arrival.

I didn't die.
I do smell.
My hair feels like oleo.
I want a shower.

It takes 3 hours and
8 phone calls
to arrange it.
A terrified teen-age
nurse's aide is told
to help me.

I promise her
I will neither
faint nor fall
nor wheeze
from this effort.

I shower.

Outside the bathroom door,
she frets.
We both survive.

She goes on her break.
I go to sleep.
Showers are exhausting.

Tuesday again – late afternoon

When we get home
Amy lights a fire
in the woodstove
and rearranges furniture
in the family room.
She shoves easy chairs
together to make
a chaise lounge.
"Mom, this room needs a sofa,"
she pants.

"I got you clean
clothes from upstairs.
If you need anything else,
let my brother get it
when he gets home.
I'll be back
in the morning
after Ben goes to school.
Wait 'til I'm here
to take a shower."

My "baby" issues orders

as she arranges parts of my dinner
beside the microwave.
Then she bundles her baby
against the cold,
we pass kisses around
and I watch the Escort's taillights
disappear into the dusk.

In the bathroom I find
a clean, soft flannel nightgown.
It buttons in front
and doesn't gape open in the back.
I take a moment
to appreciate
the utility of hospital gowns.
I appreciate more my faded flannel,
my freedom from IV lines, pumps,
and oxygen tubes.

The Spirit Within
Kristina Oliver
Honorable Mention, Images Category

Of Truth and Beauty
Arlene Barker

Truth
is a chameleon,
illusively camouflaged
with skin of deception.
Hiding in plain sight,
it stretches and slithers
through labyrinth twists.
Seekers of truth
follow the sounds
of the noisy,
but not quite clever enough
lies...
stripping them away,
revealing and restoring
the brilliance of
Truth
to its rightful beauty.

Pets
Kurt Meyer

We'd only had Hanna a couple weeks. She was a rescue whippet, twitchy and needy and nervous. But in those first two weeks she'd been so good, so obedient. Then came a Sunday dinner at my parents and we brought Hanna along. I stood in the living room with my aunt explaining Hanna's brilliance, how she never barked and never had an accident on the rug. And just as I was bragging on her – at that very moment, she (Hanna, not my aunt) squatted down and shit right there on the rug in front of us, looking up with a sorrowful apology in her eyes that would become so familiar in the years ahead.

Hanna, looking worried. Her standard expression.

Hanna only barked a few times in all the years we owned her. She slept twenty hours in a day, followed you around like a shadow for 3 hours and fifty minutes of what was left, and in that final ten minutes when you let her out to do her business, she rocketed around the yard like a bullet on crack.

There have been just a few dogs in this house, but many more cats.

Rudy came to me when I was single, left by friends who were moving out West. His original name was Yoko, but my ex-wife renamed him Rudy. He was a Siamese and smart as hell. Loved that cat.

My first house in Noblesville was the big white Victorian eventually demolished for the City Hall parking lot. We were so poor we pretty much turned off the heat at night. To stay warm, Rudy would slip under the covers up by the pillows, then burrow down to our feet. He'd get overheated and burrow back out after a while. Sometime I'd wake in the night and find him curled around your head on the pillow.

One cold winter night Rudy was burrowing out and got the covers and my ex's flannel nightgown mixed up, crawling up her gown without noticing. She woke with a frantic cat trapped against her chest, and so she was immediately frantic, unbuttoning the neck so he could get out.

I stayed home from work one day when my son Jack was 4 or 5 years old. During the morning we found Rudy had died where he often slept, curled up under my bed. He'd gone peacefully. I wrapped Rudy in an old blanket, dug a hole behind the garage and buried him, making a grave marker from a landscaping timber, spelling "Rudy" on it with a router. Jack watched all of this with fascination. When his older brother Cal got off the school bus, Jack led him to the grave and described Rudy's death and burial. Then Jack eagerly asked me if we could dig up Rudy so Cal could see.

Orion was our next cat and the baddest motherfucker to ever hunt the 1100 block alley between Maple & Cherry. He was a yellow-orange tabby with stunningly vibrant colors, had the heft of a smallish dog and looked like he'd been lifting weights. He always laid in the grass nearby when I did yard work and shared the couch each night when I relaxed with my gin and tonic. He roamed the neighborhood during the day but ran to the back door each night when I called his name.

Orion, being his bad self.

When I walked home from downtown, he'd pop out of somebody's side yard and follow me home, I'd ask him questions along the way.

"How was your day, Mr. Cat?"

"*Meow,*" he'd respond.

"Kill any chipmunks today?"

"*Meow,*" he'd call back, trotting alongside me. As long as I asked questions, he'd meow in response.

And he was forever killing rabbits and chipmunks. On a warm summer night when my daughter Sally was small, she heard a tiny, pathetic squealing in the back yard. She peered from the kitchen windows searching the yard. I went out to investigate and found Orion standing over a dying rabbit he was in the process of killing. I went back in and lied to Sally, "Orion saved us from a rat. He fought it in the back yard and thankfully Orion won."

And though Sally was our animal-lover and took to every creature she ever knew, inexplicably, Orion hated her. Perhaps he kept her at bay so she wouldn't dress him up in doll clothes. Once as he sat upright on the kitchen bench, about eye-level to Sally, she came close and reached out her hand to him. He swatted hard at her palm and she ran to me shouting excitedly, "Daddy, Orion just gave me a high-five!" How could I tell her he was really trying to scratch her eyes out? But she learned. Several times when she tried to approach him face to face he reared back with his right and coldcocked her upside the head with an open paw and bared claws. She'd come running to me in tears, stunned that an offer of kindness could result in such needless violence.

So Sally got a snuggable kitten named Nina, and though cute at first, Nina grew into the most disgusting cat I've ever known.

Nina was bullied by Orion, warning her away from the food dish until he was done eating. So when Nina got her chance she gulped food in a desperate rush. Rapidly filled with food, she'd soon vomit. She ended up on an unforgiving binge and purge cycle, so much so that even when Orion was outside and she could eat in leisure, she'd binge and purge anyway out of sheer force of habit.

But somehow she still managed to become morbidly obese: a waddling, gelatinous ball with legs and a tiny head.

You know your cat is too fat when it can't lick its own ass. Sometimes after she threw-up, she'd lie down and actually try to clean herself down there, perhaps to take the taste of vomit out of her mouth. She'd strain and struggle like a weakling trying to do a sit-up, but just couldn't reach it. This is the sort of thing that got me thinking about giving her a one-way trip to the vet.

But one day after being let out to play in the back yard, she just never came home.

And that of course is the hardest part about having pets: they die.

Orion eventually got sickly thin. Those muscular shoulders went bony. The sheen left his once brilliant coat, and he didn't hurry in when I called him at bedtime. I got to picking him up in the back yard at night and carrying him inside. But he'd still meow back if I asked him a question. Returning home from a week's vacation, the friend who was tending Orion said she hadn't seen him at all the day before we returned. I found him laying on a step halfway up the basement stairs. He was alive, but too weak to go any further. It's heartbreaking to see an old friend that way.

And that silent dog Hanna – the one that never barked? When her time came for a one-way trip to the vet, my ex-wife held her close while the vet administered the shot. As the drug pumped through her veins Hanna began to bark like she'd never barked before.

Which reveals another truth about these animals we bring into our lives. They know, see, and understand things we hardly suspect. And wondering at that mystery is perhaps the heart of the beauty of the relationship we share with them.

You Wonder
DeMaris Gaunt

You wonder
if you've ever
been imagined
into someone's day
someone's life
someone's fantasy —
have you ever
been wished
onto a plane
or into the woods
or into a warm bed
on a winter night
for a connection
that had nothing
to do with sex
and everything
to do with love —
and you wonder
if even once
you've been wanted
by the one you want —
if even once
there's been a match
in this universe
that could have
saved your life
pulled you up
and out of despair
but both of you
believed the other
deserved a kind
of perfection
out of your price range
so both of you

ended up here
on a blank page —
one of you writing
and one of you
reading into it
whatever you can.

The Cold Boy
Bill Kenley

At the start of every season we crammed a short bus to the roof with our tents, bags, food, and gear and loaded ourselves onto a big yellow Bluebird that ferried us south two hours down to the hillier, emptier, and more beautiful part of the state. There we would spend three nights in tents, playing euchre by lamplight, slapping cards down on sun-bleached wooden picnic tables, poking at glowing coals in ash-filled metal fire rings, and eating off paper plates with plastic silverware. The days were bookended by a morning run and an evening run and in between we drank gallons and gallons of Gatorade and water, threw Frisbees, played croquet and volleyball, set season goals and, ostensibly, became a more unified and focused unit as a team through the transcendent experience of simply being in nature.

The year of the cold boy, as we would call it forever after, was at the end a truly hot and humid summer. That particular first week of August, always our designated camp date, carried on the steamy momentum of June and July with a vengeance. Even at night, there was no relief. The temperature didn't seem to drop at all at sundown and dipped only to the high eighties by sunrise. That year, nobody zipped his sleeping bag. We all sweated, all the time.

I remember that first morning as we stretched on the beat-down grass in front of our tents, bending and leaning in sullen silence, sweat beading on our skin in the still air. It was almost impossible not to complain and most of us did. However, bitching was forbidden among the freshmen. They hadn't yet earned the right. The unwritten rule was you had to make it through at least one full camp session before any negativity was allowed to slip out your bacon hole. I remember that morning well, because one freshman was obnoxious and relentless in his whining. In spite of us seniors and our stink eyes and shut-ups, he refused to honor the code. His name was Jeremy Harrington.

Harrington was one of those freshmen who just didn't get it. His unwillingness to follow the no-complaints rule was just the start. He was dismissive of all our camp traditions. He acted above it all and rejected our sacred rules and rituals.

For example, for the duration of the three nights of camp, we upperclassmen insisted on cramming five or six guys in a two-man tent for the pure defiant silliness of it and encouraged the sophomores and freshmen to do the same. No fans. No air mattresses. No showers or deodorant. Maximum suffering encouraged. You truly know a guy when you spend a night in his stinky armpit, we suggested.

Most of the freshmen smiled sheepishly at us, a few enthusiastically followed our lead, but Harrington insisted on sleeping alone. That first night of camp, his little battery-powered fan hummed away in his expensive North Face tent. He complained loudly when, at lights out, the tents surrounding his were riotous with farting, slapping and giggling. He took offense at our hushed cursing, our not so subtle innuendo about our tentmates' *real* reasons for wanting to spend the night in sweaty bodily contact with four or five other teenaged boys.

He was a prude.

The second night of camp we shoved a couple of frozen hamburger patties under his tent which, as we knew they would, soon thawed and attracted a horde of raccoons who "attacked him" (his words) in the wee hours of the morning to get at the meat. That morning after Coach cooled him down and suggested he wait a day to decide whether he wanted to call his mother to come get him, he sniffingly asked for permission to move his tent away from the group. Coach granted his request with a disappointed shake of his head and a sigh.

Also, he was lazy – a useless member on his clean-up crew. That second morning after a particularly challenging trail run, he made some lame excuse about his back hurting when it was his turn to lug a cooler of water to and fro from the spigot at the edge of the campground.

I feel kind of bad ripping on him this way after what happened... I don't know.... Maybe it was the prickly and oppressive heat of that week that made us dislike him as much as we did. Probably not. He would've gotten under our skin had it been 70 and bone dry rather than 98 and so humid it felt like you were wearing a wet wool coat all the time.

Anyway, because it was so hot that week, rather than hang around the campsite during the middle of the day, reading assigned summer reading we'd put off or playing cards, we all, along with everyone else in the park, headed toward the beach, although to call it a beach would be an overstatement.

It was a strip of dark brown sand that must have been trucked in as the bottom of the lake was made up of powdery silt, no sand anywhere. The swimming area was a roped off square of tepid brownish-green water that tasted like stone and, when hundreds of swimmers were in there, was cloudy with churned up silt – impossible to see through. The swimming area was cordoned off by a scratchy hemp rope with floating buoys every ten feet or so. On the beach a bored teenaged lifeguard in a floppy tan hat and sunglasses sat under a sun-faded red umbrella on top of a rickety white lifeguard chair. It seemed, at best, a required nod to safety. The main attraction at "the beach" was a tall spiraling slide at the back of the cordoned off water.

That afternoon the little spot of lakefront was like a waterhole in a Saharan drought. You've seen the nature shows… yawning hippos, hoary wildebeests, crocodiles up to their elbows in muck, skittishly yapping hyenas, and nervous gazelles all together, no choice in the matter. On a hot day, the need for water trumps all and it felt like about a thousand of us were crammed in the warm, brown water, shoulder to shoulder, getting some relief from the chronic blast of the summer sun. I believe it was because there were so many of us swimming that day that nobody noticed the boy was missing until it was too late.

The water slide must have been the culprit, although nobody could say for sure. Harrington discovered him near the base of the slide, which made sense. The splashdown of the flume was the site of a nearly constant string of shouts and cries caused by minor injuries – kicks to the shoulder, jammed fingers, bonked noggins. Our team liked to make trains of six, seven, even ten guys, legs wrapped around each other like on a toboggan barreling down a snow-covered hill, piling up on each other in the water. Being the front man could be terrifying. There's nothing quite like being out of breath and underwater, someone's knee pressing your head down into black mucky silt, the taste of decomposing amphibian backing up into your sinuses.

The boy, I imagine he wandered too close to the slide. He got knocked out. That's my guess.

Of course, when his mother went nuts at the base of the lifeguard's chair a hushed silence spread over the water followed by whispered questions, hands over mouths in concern and fear in some cases. In others, there was excitement at the advent of some drama on an otherwise hot and dull afternoon. Her hair-tearing-out fear, her shrieking and sobbing... For me it was hard to witness. The lifeguard was clearly in over his head, no pun intended. He was just a teenager like us. It was chaos until a bearded man with an eagle tattooed on his arm, I believe it was the boy's uncle, took over.

"Make a human chain," he shouted, waving volunteers to the edge of the water. "Anyone willing to link arms! Help us!"

After we stretched from one edge of the swimming area to the other, he led us, step by step, into the murky water.

I was linked with Jeremy Harrington and was quickly disturbed to discover that he found the whole thing, well, the exact right word would be *amusing*. The wailing despair of the mother, the gung-ho heroism of the uncle, to Jeremy it all seemed like some redneck drama designed to make his otherwise unpleasant cross country camp experience tolerable. "I hope I find him," he said to me, a smirk on his face. "I've never seen a dead body before."

As we made our way out into the water, it was clear Harrington wasn't alone with his sense of gallows humor. Feeling with our toes, step after step, one woman screamed then laughed when she felt something other than lake-bottom on the sole of her foot. It turned out to be a plastic shovel. The woman laughed at the sight of the yellow plastic when the boy next to her raised it out of the water. The missing boy's mother broke down in sobs on the beach. A man glared at the woman then, and she offered an annoyed apology and said she was helping, wasn't she?

"Do you think whoever finds him will be in the paper?" Jeremy asked me, clearly hopeful at the prospect of his fifteen minutes of fame. Something turned in my stomach and I felt embarrassed to be touching him.

It's true. Connection to death fascinates some people in a most unappealing way. When a student dies – which happens every couple of years or so at a school the size of the one where I now teach – whether by suicide, accidental gunshot or car crash (those are the top three causes of teenage death by a wide margin), the desire some students have to connect to the dead always twists something in my gut.

"He was in my biology class!"

"I used to ride his bus."

"My cousin spent the night at his house once."

It's as if the deceased becomes valuable only after they're gone. A kid's popularity soars when he kicks the bucket and it's ugly if you ask me – a symptom of something wrong with either the individual or the culture or both. Whatever that wrongness is, that giddy pleasure somehow derived from being close to death but not it's chosen one, I could feel it in Jeremy Harrington. While I felt guilty and confused as I took step after step deeper into the water, quite conflicted, Harrington was excited, his eyes bright. He might have been looking for buried treasure.

Well, he found him. He got his wish. And he made the local paper, although not in a photograph as he'd hoped. Standing in the parking lot that afternoon, Harrington had asked the reporter if his picture would be on the front page. When the young woman said no, he argued his case as if he'd been denied something legitimately his like a spoiled little boy refused a treat. Harrington seemed to think himself a hero for finding the dead boy's body. He seemed to consider touching the five-year-old's lifeless body curled on the bottom of the lake with his foot a sign of bravery on his part. I think his sense of his own heroism was why the boy visited him that night, although I'll never truly know.

One thing I do know about ghosts is why they're ghosts. A ghost is a spirit that has refused to or can't move on to the next world, wherever and whatever that world is. Some ghosts suffer such trauma at their own demises that they don't know they're dead. It's a form of denial. Other ghosts know they are no longer among the living, but a desire for revenge or redemption dictates that they wander the earth like Marley's ghost or haunt their own particular corner of it. I think, based on what Jeremy told us that third morning of camp, that the boy didn't even know he was dead. He was cold, lonely and confused.

That third morning, as we silently stretched in the heat, Jeremy had to be roused from his tent. As Coach berated him, shouting through the dark netting that was the door, finally letting rip with his pent-up frustration at him, Jeremy barely seemed to notice. He slowly unzipped his tent and pushed back the flap lethargically, his eyes down. Rather than argue or make excuses, he was totally silent. As he made his way towards us, he looked dazed and sick. His eyes wouldn't focus. He didn't say a word as we stretched. Then, as we jogged out towards the trails, I saw wetness on his cheeks. And it wasn't sweat. He was crying.

We all stood there then, the heat of the morning sun bouncing up off the asphalt. We made a circle with him in the middle. We asked him what was wrong. Eyes down, he told us the drowned boy was in his tent. He said he was in his sleeping bag. Bit by bit, we got the details.
In the deepest dark of the night, Jeremy said he woke up to the sound of water dripping. He heard a voice then – a little boy's voice, high and thin and scared. Jeremy unzipped his door to find the drowned boy standing there shivering in the moonlight in a wet pair of swimming trunks. As he began to describe the boy, he became overwrought and couldn't speak. We all knew why. We'd all seen him stretched out on a gurney, his skin blue, his lips purple like two thin worms dead in a puddle. It was an awful vision, one I tried hard to get out of my mind, although I doubt I ever will. Then he described the boy squatting down and crawling on his hands and knees into his tent.

There was a coldness radiating off of him. Like a powerful fever except his skin was cold rather than hot. He was leaking dark lake water. It was coming out of his nose and the corners of his eyes, which Jeremey described as no longer having any whites. Pulsing streams escaped the edges of his mouth when he spoke. "He was a little boy, just a five-year-old, probably not four feet tall and under fifty pounds," said Jeremy in a shaky voice full of something we'd never heard from him before.

"What did he want," I asked, my voice hushed. The morning bugs trilled in the rising heat of the day.

Jeremy looked at me then. His eyes were full of anguish. They were the eyes of someone whose learned an awful secret and can't ever unknow it.

"He said, 'I'm cold.'" Jeremy wrapped his arms around himself. "He said 'Hold me. Make me warm.'" A little choke came out of his throat. He shook his head and his mouth crumpled up. "And I did…" Then he grabbed my arm and his eyes bored into mine. I was so startled I jumped back, but I couldn't break away from his grip. "I couldn't make him warm!" He shook his head. "I tried!" He let go of my arm then, his voice dropped so it was barely audible. He was speaking only to himself. "I couldn't…"

Of course, we all thought Jeremy had just lost it. A bad dream. Maybe the beginnings of a conscious in a kid who clearly needed one, but when we got back from our run, Jeremy wouldn't go near his tent. He sat on a post all the way across the campground. Finally, a couple of the other seniors and I decided we had to check it out.

I have to admit, when we were crouched down in front of that tent way off away from all the others, I swear I could hear some kind of raspy, burbling noise, kind of like when you're sick and your lungs are full of gook. But when I unzipped the door and pulled it aside, there was nobody there.

But something was off. It was Harrington's sleeping bag. It was soaking wet.

I didn't want to touch it, but something made me. The need to know the truth is strong, and I pulled his soaking sleeping bag across the bottom of the tent and lifted it up to my face. I sniffed it. It was as I'd feared. The smell, it wasn't urine and it wasn't the iodine tang of salt mixed with body-odor, the smell of sweat. It had a distinct smell, a mineral smell. It smelled like the bottom of the lake.

That afternoon Coach took Jeremy Harrington into the nearest town and called his parents from a pay phone. They came and got him. He quit the team. That morning was the last time he ran with us.

Over the course of that year at school, he became something of a ghost himself. I heard from some of his fellow freshmen that he didn't speak in his classes, and when I passed him in the hallways he wouldn't make eye contact. He had the pallid, gaunt look of an addict, like something was stealing his energy. One time I did get him to talk to me. After sitting down uninvited at a lunch table where he sat in solitude, I asked him if he was okay. He lethargically pushed a limp green bean around his plate with a fork. It was only when I asked if what had happened at camp still bothered him that he raised his eyes from his plate and met mine.

Every night, he told me, the drowned boy came to him. Every night he would hear the sound of dripping water on the carpet next to his bed. And every night, he would take the boy into his arms in an attempt to warm him up, but the boy would never warm up. He just shivered and radiated that deep chill he couldn't shake off. Just before daylight, he would go away.

"And then he comes back the next night," said Jeremy. His eyes were, as they say, drowning. He turned his attention away from me and back to his plate. "I don't know where he goes in between," he whispered. And he wasn't talking to me anymore.

About three weeks after I spoke to him, Jeremy Harrington was discovered in his garage, hanging from a noose at the end of a rope looped and knotted around a rafter, a stool overturned at his feet. After his suicide, Leonardo rounded us all up down in our locker room and told us we should go to his funeral.

Keane replied that we knew Leonardo had hated Harrington. He, among all of us, had chafed hardest against Harrington's whining and lack of toughness, his unwillingness to attempt to be one of us. Why, he asked, would he want us to go to something as sad as the funeral of a teenage suicide we'd never really known?

Leonardo was profoundly Catholic with a bit of El Salvadoran superstition thrown in. He stared at Keane for a moment. "You want to hear a dripping sound on your bedroom floor some night?" he asked. "You want to take over?"

We went to the funeral.

Some nights I wake up thinking of Jeremy Harrington and the cold boy. I wonder where they are. Did the boy move on to the next world? Heaven? Was his soul connected in some way to Harrington's? Is it Jeremy's soul that wanders now? As far as I know, nobody on our team ever received a visit from the boy.

And every year when August arrives and season kicks in again, I think of all those young runners at camp. I wonder if any of them have ever been awakened by the sound of dripping water. I wonder if they've unzipped their tents in the middle of the night to see a cold little boy standing there shivering, looking for someone to hold him through the night, someone to make him warm. Or maybe it's not a little boy standing there in the dark dripping black water. Maybe it's a haunted fifteen-year-old with a red, raw, bruised ring around his neck looking for solace.

Vibrations in VII
Celeste Williams

2018 *Award of Merit*
(our *Best in Book* award)

I.

Trayvon
and Sandra
and Jimmie Lee
and Emmett

they are like lyrics we know

and Michael
and Martin
and Medgar

lyrics we know by heart.

and Viola
and Malcolm
and Philando

their names vibrate

and Tamir
and Eric
and the Charleston Nine

vibrate like a plucked string

and Goodman
and Schwerner
and Cheney

the shudder after a thrum
and Addie Mae

and Cynthia

and Carole
and Denise

II.

Memory.
A thread drawn taut,
reaching back farther than we
can see —

It is said that Ancestors
hold the plectrum
that releases a tone

all that is known
and not yet known —
a note that should be heeded.

But memory triggers
painful hymns,
rolling sea-billows of sorrows

that signal that no —
no, it is not well with my soul.
Because the vibration

is never-ending
and travels the
infinite length of that string

III.

A mother calls police
about a man
who manhandled her young son

and she is tackled
and taken to jail.
It takes me instantly back

to a white security guard's
hands clenched on my arms
in a department store.

In my mother's eyes, I see
fierceness
and fear.

Emmett's mother said
leave the coffin
lid open.

"I wanted the world
to see what they did
to my baby."

IV.

Emmett Till's accuser
said in 2016
that she lied about

the details
of the 1955 event
that incited

the disfiguring torture
and murder
of Mamie Till's baby boy.

Some of us
weren't born yet
but still we remember.

Like flashbacks
Medgar Evers' widow
had upon hearing

the sounds
of a certain
candidate's rallies.

V.

In 2017 Georgia
a police chief
gives a rare apology

for a lynching
that happened
in 1940.

He apologizes
to the black people —
many who

weren't alive then
but they
never forgot. He says

"There are relatives here
and people
who still remember.

Even if those people
are not still alive,
down through

the generations
that memory
is still alive."

VI.

Erica Garner
was named for
her father, Eric

who told the police

who were choking him
that he couldn't breathe.

And he died.

Erica spoke out
until she could
no longer breathe.

And she died.

VII.

Vibrations, hymns
go on and on and on…
No, it is not well
with my soul.

Chicago is vibrating
Indianapolis is vibrating
America is vibrating.

echoes of
dissonant notes,
memory

known and
not yet known

lived and
not yet lived.

Trayvon
and Sandra
and Jimmie Lee
and Emmet

and

Looking Up
DeMaris Gaunt

Tug of War
DeMaris Gaunt

Today
you will be expected
to demonstrate
your genetic fortitude
while you get the work done
efficiently and well
and you will be expected
to laugh at the jokes
made by your father
at the expense
of your mother
when she's not around
and you will do this
with an effort so great
it will appear effortless
and later on
you will be expected
to use the manners
you learned as a child
while you listen
to your mother rehash
the past forty years
of emotional neglect
which was worth it
she swears
because she got you
so you listen
with a detached disgust
that's replaced your empathy
making sure the lines
in your furrowed brow
appear authentic
because you
are on the payroll

and your job
isn't damage control
your job is
favorite child
and you're going for gold
on two accounts.

The Sound of Echoes

Crystal Morrison

"Atlanta Center, this is N344A requesting assistance."

The hair on the back of Steve's neck stood on end as the panicked voice reverberated through his headset. He quickly replied to the caller as he searched his Atlanta center control terminal for an unidentified blip.

"Go ahead, N344A, say request."

"N344A requesting flight following. I've gotten off course and feel a little disoriented. I'm a VFR pilot and the conditions up here are deteriorating fast," replied the rattled voice.

"Not a problem N344A, try to maintain visual flight conditions and squawk 3256," Steve calmly instructed from the dark radar room.

"Roger," said the voice with an audible sense of relief, "I'm tuning my transponder to 3256 and am at an altitude of 6,500 feet."

Within seconds Steve saw the now-identified blip and responded, "N344A I have you on my radar. Looks like you are 22 miles east of the Athens, GA airport. Say destination, type of aircraft, and equipment please."

There was a long eerie silence before the pilot responded, "My final destination? I just want to see my family."

Steve didn't expect this kind of answer, but stress can make people respond in odd ways, so taking his training into account, Steve cautiously replied, "Understood N344A, what is your flight destination for today? Which airport are you meeting your family?"

Seeming more agitated and distracted, the pilot replied, "I departed Daniel Field in Augusta, Georgia in my Cessna 172 for Blairsville, Georgia airport. The identifier is Kilo-Delta-Zulu-Juliet."

Annotating this new information, Steve directed, "Roger that N344A, let's fly heading of 315 degrees and maintain 6,500 feet. Based on your radar position, that should get you going in the direction of your destination. Do you have a GPS on board?"

There was another odd silence and then the once panicked pilot almost seemed to be smirking or smiling as he dryly replied, "Yes, turning to a heading of 315 degrees, and I'm still searching for my destination."

In today's modern age, a pilot heading out any decent distance from his hometown airport without a GPS was ludicrous. Steve shook his head in frustration as he contemplated the older sounding gentleman flying around in a small aircraft with minimal instrumentation and deteriorating weather conditions. He tried to shake the prickling sensation running down his spine.

Steve's workload increased and his screen filled up with a menagerie of blips and data. He was busy attending the other various aircraft coming in and out of the Atlanta airspace when the small Cessna burst in again on the frequency.

This time the pilot's panic was back tenfold as he exclaimed, "Atlanta Center, N344A – the clouds have closed in completely underneath me and I no longer have visual on the ground. The cloud deck above me seems to be lowering. How much longer until I can descend? How many more miles from my current position do you see me from Blairsville?"

Fighting back an ominous feeling, Steve replied with authority, "N344A, you are still on course and are still on my scope. You are 48 miles from the Blairsville, GA airport. Descend and maintain 5,500 feet. That is the minimum descent altitude due to mountainous terrain. I cannot bring you any lower at this point. Please maintain 5,500 feet."

Not really answering Steve, the frustrated pilot retorted, "It's always like this. It's always the same outcome."

Even though he was maintaining his heading and altitude, this guy was clearly unraveling.

Steve broke in and said, "N344A, I repeat, you are on course. Please maintain your current heading and altitude."

There was no reply. Steve hated to do it, but it was time to bring in Dan. Dan was on as shift supervisor; and he was already a guy wound way too tight. July 2 was Atlanta's hottest day so far in 2016. Of course, the center's air conditioning was out in the radar room, and tensions were high. As much as Steve dreaded it, his instincts were screaming for him to bring this poor pilot to Dan's attention.

Signaling for him, Dan came over and Steve brought him up to speed. They looked at the blip on the screen and noted the pilot seemed to be holding heading and altitude fine. The weather he was describing must simply be the heat-of-the-day cloud buildups. It was certainly hot and humid enough to make a bubbling cauldron of clouds and potential rain out there.

"It's odd though," Steve said, "no one else is mentioning any difficulties with the weather. Even my VFR pilots out there are able to maintain in the clear. I've asked multiple others if they're seeing anything and the answer is no. He's in some high terrain, and I'm not going to be able to step him down for another 20 miles."

Almost transfixed and unusually calm, Dan said, "Talk to him, Steve. We'll hand off your other planes. Have him switch to a private frequency and see if you can get him to calm down a bit. I've got an odd feeling about this one."

Nodding in complete agreement, Steve adjusted his scope to zoom in on the Cessna.

Grabbing a notepad and pen, he keyed for a new frequency and contacted the pilot, "N344A, switch to my frequency on 132.35 please."

The pilot checked in on the new frequency.
Relieved, Steve ventured, "You're doing great and still right on course, N344A. My name is Steve, what's yours? How long have you been flying?"

"My name is Ellis and I've been flying for what seems too long now."

Before Steve could reply to this incredibly odd statement, the pilot's tone changed completely as he asked in a clipped voice, "What are you painting on your screen? It's getting really dark. How bad does the rain I'm in look on your scoop?"

Steve searched the scoop in vain, "Ellis, I'm not painting any rain on my radar in your area. I know you said you were in and out of the clouds now, perhaps it's just their intense moisture."

"This isn't going to end well for me," Ellis said distractedly. "It was imperative I was there to see my family. Steve, I'm a realist. If something happens, make sure they know I said goodbye. Can you make sure of that for me?"

Rattled, Steve suddenly felt cold in the sweltering control room.

"Of course Ellis, but don't talk like that," Steve managed to say. "We're gonna get you safely to your family. Now, I need you to maintain that heading and step down 1000 feet for me. Maintain that 4,500 feet for just a few more miles. You're only 23 miles from the airport. Soon as we get you under that cloud deck, you'll pop out and see that beautiful landing site. It'll be like heaven. Keep the faith...we can do this."

"Keep the faith?" Ellis asked dryly. "I do have hope though. That's why I keep trying."

He just stopped. Ellis just stopped and it was silent as a tomb on the radio. The blip on his screen was gone. Steve rubbed his eyes to clear his vision. What just happened? Ellis had just vanished off his screen.

Steve keyed the mike, "N344A, how do you hear? Ellis, this is Steve – do you copy?"

Nothing...there was no reply...nothing but the droning sound of the obnoxious box fan whirring and stirring the hot air.

Steve sent countless transmissions to Ellis over what seemed the longest ten minutes of his life. No answer, no blip on the scope, and the silence just echoed in his headset.

Steve hadn't noticed Dan had left his side and returned, so it startled him when Dan touched his shoulder and said in a comforting tone, "I've got it called in. His fate is in God's hands now."

Steve looked at Dan blankly, but his mind swirled as he tried to process what Dan just said.

Search and rescue were immediately dispatched to comb every trajectory from the last know fix. The NTSB questioned everyone in the radar room that day and confiscated the tapes. Tom White was the lead investigator and an old friend of Steve's. Tom promised he'd be in touch with any word.

Days upon days went by with no information. The news didn't run a story; and there were no articles in the paper. Steve tried to concentrate at work, but he couldn't get Ellis' panicked voice out of his head. Five days later, Tom finally showed up at the center. Dan led him over to Steve's console and told him he'd cover his scope so Tom and he could talk. Grateful and apprehensive, he handed the headset to Dan and led Tom to the little conference room down the hall.

"Steve, I'm a man of science and a skeptic, but I'm scratching my head on this one," Tom said as he exhaled a big sigh. "It's been seventy-two hours and they've called off the search. There was no crash site, no eyewitness reports, and nothing showed on their readouts. It's as if this craft just vanished into thin air; it's as if it never existed."

"But Tom, you heard the tapes. You know where he was; we had a strong fix on him. Plus, at his altitude he should never have fallen off my scope. It doesn't make any sense," Steve exclaimed. "I felt his panic and confusion. What about all those cryptic things he said about goodbyes? What about all those ramblings about his destination?"

"I know, Steve," Tom said cautiously as he cleared his throat. "You'd better brace yourself for this one. It gets grayer. We talked to the staff at Daniel Field. They didn't know that plane and had no record of anyone departing the airport that afternoon. When I started entering my preliminary data into the NTSB accident database, N344A was already in there."

Tom took a deep breath and looked him dead in the eyes as he continued.

"Steve, on July 2, 1976 – exactly 40 years from the date of this incident – a small aircraft departed near Augusta, GA for Blairsville, GA. The sole occupant crashed *en route* in the North Georgia mountains. The report cited pilot error due to continued flight into instrument conditions and extremely adverse weather. The VFR pilot was listed as Ellis Jones and the tail number was N344A."

Steve went as white as a sheet, as Tom went on, "I don't believe in coincidence and I'm not sure where to take this investigation from here. Steve, it's as if you were talking to the sound of echoes."

Movie Magic

Sam Watermeier

The film flickered
like the kicking feet inside her.
A boy,
galled by *The Godfather III*,
was ready to exit the theater …
and her womb.

The father wanted to stay
for the climactic scene.
But the light of the projector
was no match for his wife's eyes.

They rushed to the hospital
where they met their bundle
of hair as black as Michael Corleone's.
"Let's name him Superman," their other son said.
"He'll be Superman one day,
but let's not pressure him," the parents replied.
"Clark will be his middle name
until he can fly."

Soon they took the boy home,
a gift that cut the winter chill.
(He had superpowers already!)
Now, outside of movie theaters,
they could see that magic was real.

The Banned Book
Susan Hoskins Miller
First Prize, Song Lyric/Poetry Category

In the coffee house on the town square, we took turns reading aloud
from the book banned by the school board, censored for the erotic fantasy
that swept through one character's mind, as if such ideas would never occur
to those high school readers, they with their riotous hormones.

One of those students joined us on that day. He settled into the leather chair,
opened the book and read words forbidden to him, while his parents looked on.
One by one, others read:
A mother
a lawyer
a plumber
a neighbor
a business owner
a cook,
and people passing by,
lending their many voices so that intellectual freedom could live in America
for one more day.

NOTE: On Jun. 24, 2002, the Noblesville School Board, Noblesville, Indiana, voted to ban the book, "Follow the River," by Hoosier author, James Alexander Thom. The book had been on the required reading list at Noblesville High School until one parent complained about one scene in Chapter 27. Parents lobbied the board to reinstate the book on the reading list to no avail. A few weeks later, the Indiana chapter of the American Civil Liberties Union hosted a marathon reading of the book at Noble Coffee and Tea to protest the board's action.

Crawl Space Beer

Casey Kenley

The six of us girls were packed into the car, sweat fogging the windows, even with the windows down. I was driving. The Violent Femmes blared *Blister in the Sun* on the tape player over our shrieks. Cans of Milwaukee's Best popping open, sloshing around in the back seat. It was a perfect summer high school night.

Off the highway, down the road a bit and past the fence line, we turned into the driveway, the quarter-mile dip and the climb to my house in the country. But the porch light was on. I hadn't left it on. I shoved on the breaks and the girls went silent. Someone hit the off button and the music died.

"They know," I said.

They must know. Our headlights would be the only light for half a mile, and it was only eight o'clock. They weren't in bed yet. But they were supposed to be a hundred miles away, on a date in Memphis. They never left me all by myself for a night, so I'd invited the girls for a sleepover, and lots of beer.

We'd bought it after school that afternoon. Tracy's fake ID always worked at that quick stop on Highland Avenue. I hauled it all home and brought it inside after Mom and Dad had left for the night. The beer we intended to consume filled the fridge. And when the fridge was full, I had stashed it in cabinets in cast iron skillets and saucepans. I even put a few six packs in the crawl space under the house.

The jig was up. That was pretty obvious. We were sixteen and scared, but at least we had our story straight: *We weren't going to leave the house. We were going to be safe and drink at home. It was stupid. No, we don't do this often. We're so, so sorry. It will never happen again.* I parked the car and we all slid out. The girls followed me inside with their sleeping bags, quiet as cats when cats want to be invisible.

"Casey?" she called from upstairs.

"Hey, Mom. I thought y'all were spending the night," I called back.

Her footfalls down the stairs didn't sound like they carried the weight of an angry mom. She flipped on the kitchen light.

"Well, we just decided to call it an early night," she said, blinking under the lights and looking past me. "What are you girls doing?"

She appeared curious, not accusing, as my five friends stood behind me, gripping their sleeping bags. Maybe the tighter they squeezed the less severe the punishment would feel. I strayed from our story, hoping my instinct was right.

"We didn't really have any plans so I said we could come back here," my voice shook. Mom tilted her head, blinked once. "And watch a movie or something. Just spend the night."

"Well, have fun. Don't be too loud. Dad and I called it an early night. We're going to bed," Mom said and went back upstairs.

They hadn't opened a cabinet. They hadn't opened the fridge. They had no idea the level of loudness and drunkenness we planned to reach on cheap light beer.

A few weeks later, a safe distance from our brush with a permanent grounding from sleepovers, Mom was banging silverware. She clanged a cookie sheet into a cabinet.

"You OK, Mom?"

"It's Josh. Dad was doing some work under the house and he found beer," she said.

She was pissed. My heart leapt. That night, after we had stealthily pulled all the beer out of the kitchen and put it back in the trunk of my car, I had forgotten about the crawl space.

"Oh," I said. That's all I said. Until years later.

My brother always got in trouble. Or at least he always got caught. I was the middle child, two years younger than Josh, five years older than our sister Ally. I followed along with my brother as our parents moved us from public to private to public and then back to private schools as my parents tried to find the right school for Josh. I got good grades, covered my tracks and looked – at least from the outside – to be a "pleaser." Josh got bad grades, a DUI, and could be moody. I'm sure I was hard to live with.

Years later, when I told Josh that I had been the one who forgot to get the beer out of the crawl space, he didn't even remember the incident. And he didn't care.

Did it matter that I didn't own up to it? Probably not. But I remember it because, while most of the grief my brother brought on himself was due to his own behavior, this one I caused and it wasn't his fault.

Today, Josh and I have a good relationship. We call each other at least once a month. When I bring my kids to visit my parents' house, he hand-ties lures and fishes with my boys. I think he forgives me for being the good kid. We both still like beer.

Just East of Those Western Parts
Rachel Cox

Just east of those Western parts,
where the mountains fade
and the land yawns out like
a poorly remembered hymn,
there is a place.

Lightning bugs, not fireflies, twinkle
in my silver-etched memory,
their buzz against my palm
as rich as a grandfather's laughter.

The somnolent croak of the toads
dances
with the pulsating roar of the cicadas,
that true Nachtmusik.

These things twist and flutter
in my past,
framed by storybook summer skies
and clinking noises from
inside a neighbor's house.

Sometimes I dream of them,
of candlelight through the sycamores
still glowing my way
Home

Then I rise and sing:
North of the river,
South of the lake,
I pray the Lord
my soul to take.

Tiny Dancer
DeMaris Gaunt

If Looks Could Kill

Maren Thornbury

There's a boy in my class who doesn't like to talk
He doesn't have a bag or books or a pen.
But when I pass him his test it always says one hundred percent.
The teacher could tap his shoulder when he closes his eyes
and he wouldn't flinch,
and if asked a question he knows the answer to all he'd say is a blink.

I know a boy in my school whose teeth were never straight, but he had
perfect vision and a wonderful splash of freckles on his nose.
One day I found him sitting outside with silent waterfalls pooling in his
amber eyes, his face was rubbed raw and bleeding where his freckles used
to shine,
I helped him clean up, but when I asked him why all he could say was a
shake of his head.
When he walked away there was a limp in his step and I cried for his
beautiful skin.

Sometimes I sit with a boy in my town, whose bones are paper thin,
and I tell him old jokes and poems I wrote on the back of chocolate milk
cartons.
He may try to pretend he doesn't know I'm there, or that he doesn't
comprehend, but yesterday when the flags were half-mast
and I was choking back tears,
he reached over to squeeze my hand.
I saw in his eyes a smile he probably couldn't tell was there, so I thanked
him over and over again for listening and letting me be his friend.

Days ago this boy in my neighborhood threw up on the side of the road,
then he threw rocks at plastic cups until night turned to dawn and dawn
turned to dusk.
I sat at my window with some chicken noodle soup, and watched him
cough up his lungs,
and my heart broke for the boy on the street screaming for "someone to
see me!"
There are some things in life we can never forgive ourselves for,
and that night listening to a drowning kid trying to hold his head above
water, but never leaving my bed, I adopted guilt as a lifelong pet.

Because

there was a boy in my class who didn't like to talk,
and glared at everyone passing him by.
He was small and pale and thin, and his bones could be heard crunching
wherever he went.
I only read him old jokes and poems on backs of chocolate milk cartons,
but we are bitter children who crave attention and I gave up before I could
wallow.
If looks could kill, I died every day when that boy bore sad eyes into my
own.
"Just talk to me" I'd think, too full of shame and longing for a kid I'd
never really know.
The boy didn't speak and he didn't laugh and he didn't smile,
he stayed out all night in the freezing cold without a jacket on, throwing
up in bushes and coughing up organs.

Then one day in December, before school let out and Christmas fantasies
filled our heads,
the boy didn't come back inside.
And for three days no one knew where he was, no one cared...
Until the dogs found his body by the tree he used to climb when he was
young and little and still smiled all the time,
frozen and stiff and with blood stained puke stuck to the side of his cheek.
I sat on the bench where I read him old jokes and stories I wrote when I
was sad, and I cried for a boy who would never listen again.
They flew the flags at half mast for less than a week, and at the funeral
nobody came
to weep for a child that we never truly cared about, to weep without
knowing his name.
I decided to speak at the service, words from the only "friend" he might
have had.
I wrote the eulogy on a jug of chocolate milk, and read a poem I saved
just for him.

"There's a boy in my class who doesn't like to talk
He doesn't have a bag or books or a pen.
but when I pass him his test it always says one hundred percent...."

A Serengeti Sunset in Central Indiana
Sam Watermeier
Tie for *Third Place*, Images Category

Photographer's Note: When I took this photo, I didn't feel like I captured an ordinary Indiana sunset. I felt as if I were transported to the jungles of Africa. What was once familiar suddenly seemed otherworldly. I learned that if you look closely, there is plenty of magic within the mundane.

Listen

Rachel Cox

Listen for the whisper
for the creak, for the sigh
the small exhale of breath
alerting the presence of
Another

You are not alone
as you wish to be
as you hate to be
Yearning for
the freedom of only you
Dreading only yourself

Sunrise Sunset
Annie Oberman

Footloose on Freedom Lane

Gail Geisler

The ground is flying by in front of the bike and the wind is blowing my hair. We are heading to the store and I'm happy and free on the handlebars of my sister's bike, my feet in my worn Red Ball Jets squeezing the hub of the front wheel like a cowgirl's knees squeeze her horse. I'm too young to ride a two-wheeler, but Karen is three years older and confident as we race along. It's a cool morning, and I smell the freshly cut grass. It's not hot yet, but it will be by afternoon.

Nowhere to be, Mom at work for the day, my older siblings in charge, this is my summer. Free to explore this neighborhood or the next, using a back way to get to the corner store with its penny candy, my pocket filled with change and my library card. Maybe we'll see the bookmobile!

We turn at the farmhouse on the corner of our dirt road and follow the broken narrow sidewalk, avoiding the busy road where Mom won't let us ride. We race over the lone step along the sidewalk, and for a moment we really are flying. Then in an instant we're sprawled on the ground, a tangle of arms and legs. I see blood by Karen's head and I'm terrified. I think the blood is coming out of her head, and maybe some brains, too? Slowly we untangle ourselves, right the bike, and determine that no brains have leaked out. It's the top of my foot that's bleeding. And it hurts. My foot must have slipped into the spokes of the front wheel as we bumped down the step and sent us cantilevering over the handlebars. I stand, but I feel sharp pain if I put weight on my right foot. I can't walk. I have to get back on the handlebars to ride back home, more hesitantly this time.

The day goes by slowly. I really can't get around, but I'm bored being inside. When friends stop by to get me, I put my arm over a shoulder and hop to their house. It's always more fun at someone else's house. We go to Lynn's and hang out with her mom. I watch the cigarette smoke curl and the ashes grow as Doris talks - she wants me to call her Doris! She wears a sleeveless shell and pedal pushers; her flip-flops slap the linoleum floor when she walks. She makes chicken and dumplings for dinner. I'm fascinated by the Bisquick dough dropping into the pot of canned chicken noodle soup, sputtering away on the steamy stove. We don't make this at our house. She gives me a taste of the warm gooey dumpling before sending me on my way. Time for them to eat, and me to go. Alone now, I alternate between hopping and crawling through the neighborhood, slowly heading home.

Then I see my Mom, home from work after another long day, looking weary in her uniform and worn polished white shoes.

When she sees me, I see something flash in her eyes. I think she's mad. And she never gets mad. I try to figure out what's wrong, struggling to understand what I did. I decide that she's upset because I'm crawling. Maybe it's embarrassing, for the neighbors to see me crawling?

"Gail, what happened? Are you OK?"

I quickly jump up, explaining, "It's OK, Mom. I was also hopping, not just crawling. Mostly I hopped!"

Her face is flushed and she has tears in her eyes. "Why didn't anyone call me?"

After a hurried dinner we head to the hospital emergency room. That was the summer I learned to use crutches.

I grew up in a rural subdivision outside Flint, Michigan, the youngest of four kids. I actually lived on Freedom Lane in Independence Villa, aptly describing my childhood. My parents were both WWII vets who met as students at the University of Michigan. They divorced when I was three and my mom worked as a dental hygienist, raising four kids as a single mom in the early 1960s. She was the only Mom I knew who worked, and I didn't meet anyone else with divorced parents for many years. I was acutely aware that we were different. With no extended family nearby for support, life was hard but my mother seemed capable and strong to me. My summers were full of unsupervised adventure and freedom.

It wasn't until much later that I could understand her frustration. Summers were fun for us, but rough on my mom. Trying to be a good parent to four young kids, and doing it alone, was tough. Leaving us at home all day with my twelve-year-old brother in charge was a necessity but always a looming worry. Arriving home in the evening and seeing that your five-year-old couldn't walk and no one had bothered to tell you, was devastating. Dinner still needed to be made, then a trip to the hospital emergency room, and tomorrow would bring another early morning.

Somehow, she managed it all with grace and determination. I think that's what she taught me – you just put one foot in front of the next, figure it out, and press on. What else could you do?

Broken Mirrors
Vivian Belle

Back then
my eyes were bright
Back then
my smile was easy
Back then
my skirts were tight

Back then
my legs were tan
Back then
my hair was golden
Back then
when life began

Back then
I didn't think ahead
Back then
the days just passed
Back then
there was no dread

Back then
no one warned me
Back then
I didn't know
Back then
I couldn't see

the old woman
in the broken mirror
staring back at me

Perch'n on Lake Michigan 2017
Al Geisler

My brother, Dave, and I were out fishing on Lake Michigan one evening in September. We caught our limit of perch in 50 feet of water about 5 miles south of the South Haven pier heads. After sunset it was time to head in and try our luck for something bigger. Dave started up the engine on the Lund and hit the gas for shore. Our Lund is the 18' Fishermen with a 165Hp Chevy V-6 inboard. It is set up with gear for trolling the big lake. Big Jon rod trees for running planners, track mounted rod holders for running Dipsies, three downriggers capable of running 9 down rods when including sliders. There is a bow-mounted Minn Kota wireless trolling motor and a 15Hp Mercury Big Foot kicker to hold the Lund on speed and course. We use a Fish Hawk X4 sensor to locate the thermocline, monitor water temps, and find the correct speed and direction relative to the variable bottom currents of the big lake.

The salmon run was just getting started and we had the Ugly Stiks & Power rods all rigged and ready for the big one. My favorite 12ft rod was set with 20lb mono on an old Cardinal 6 reel that my fish'n buddy Ray Motluck gave me. It might be the "Luck" on that reel that always produces a big fish each time out on the water. As we approached the pier heads, about ½ mile away, Dave cut back on the gas. It was fully dark and the lights from the south pier and South Haven shore line twinkled with beauty. The city police were searching the South Beach. You could see a 4-wheeler driving along the water's edge with spot-lights searching the dune grass for something or someone.

"What do you think the cops are looking for, Dave?"

"Don't know, but something's up for them to be all the way down by the blue stairs."

We watched as the spot light panned back and forth and up and down the bluff. Feeling a bit careless about their search, it's not an issue for us, we are over a mile off shore. Nothing out here to bother us.

I decide to cast my rod baited with a blue and silver Loco I had recovered from a snag while fishing the Manistee river the week prior. It's an old proven lure that was a hot bait in the 70's when the King Salmon ran heavy up the Black River. Just after setting the rod in a holder, a fish hit the Loco and had the Power rod bent over. The line was ripping off the spool as the fish made a first run.

After about 50 yards of line stripped, Dave said, "You need to tighten the drag and get that fish to turn. Get him turned with the boat."

I knew I had plenty of line to fight out this fish, however Dave was correct, so I tightened the drag. The rear internal drag is one of the features that made this Cardinal reel so famous. The other being the 6:1 retrieve ratio, designed to keep tight lines when a fish makes a direct run back at you. Before I was able to turn the fish, it jumped and broke water with a big splash on the surface. You could tell it was a huge monster. It took off and ripped more line from the reel. The fish then went deep for the bottom and finally turned with the boat. I started to gain line and slowly brought the fish in closer to the boat. It stayed down close to the bottom and was almost directly under the boat.

Dave yelled, "Don't let it cut the line in the motor."

Just then the fish raced up from the bottom of the lake. It made a fast run directly up under the boat. That fish was trying to slack line me and drop the hook. I cranked as fast as I could on that old Cardinal but I was unable to keep the line tight. The line went slack and apparently the fish shook the hook. Another big one that got away! Or did it???

I started to hear a voice.

"Do you hear that? What is it? Dave, did you turn on the radio or is that your phone?"

Dave responded, confused, "I don't know."

He stood up from the driver's seat to take a look.

Dave announced in amazement, "There's something hanging on the front of our boat!"

In disbelief, I quickly move to the front of the boat to have a look. There was a dark shadow of a face and arms holding on to the front of the Lund. The body dragged thru the water like a very large fish under the boat. Dave immediately cut back the gas and turned off the engine.

I shouted out, "Dude! What are you doing?"

Fish-Man replied, "I fell out of my boat."

Sure, right, there's no boat around here.

"Where's your boat? How long have you been in the water?"

"Over an hour. I have been swimming and looking for my boat."

"OK, swim to the back of the boat where we can get you out of the water."

He swam along the side of the boat. Sizing him up, the landing net was not big enough, so I grabbed him under the armpit like landing a big fish by the gills. When I lifted him up into the Lund, he was a big'n! Maybe 6'-5" to 6'-7". I looked up at Fish-Man to more carefully size him up. I'd put him around a 260-270 pounder, a solid muscular build.

Then, Dave started to giggle, "He's naked! He's totally naked!!!"

I didn't look down to confirm, there was no need to confirm this fact. I just took two backward steps and thought this might be a bad situation. We just landed some naked man-fish and had no idea of his intentions. Was he a good fish or a bad man? Was he the slippery & slimy fish the cops were trolling for along the shore? He had somehow jumped back into the water and got away in the lake by the dark of night! How are we going to throw him back? If this gets ugly, it could be a bad situation, like a bad catch and release. I could use a weapon. Maybe something to hit him on the head. Something to stun this Fish-man before he starts flopping around in the boat. Dave was thinking the same thing and was standing behind me, waiting to see how this was going to play out. I did not notice but Dave had grabbed his fillet knife. It's a razor-sharp twenty-inch heavy steel blade he uses to fillet the biggest fish we catch. Dave had the knife behind his back and was ready to take action if necessary.

I asked Fish-Man again, what happened? He replied that he was working on his boat lights and fell overboard. The boat drove away without him. He was trying to swim fast, however was not fast enough.

"It went out of sight going that way." Fish-Man said, pointing south.

It was cold, so we offered a heavy 3X size sweatshirt and my winter bibs. For some reason Fish-Man was unable to put them on. He just threw them over his shoulders and wrapped them around his waist.

I asked Fish-Man, "How long have you been swimming?"

He said for probably over an hour, that initially he could see the light on his boat.

"It went that way." Again he pointed south toward Deerlick Creek.

I told him we just came from that direction and saw no boat.

"Have you been drinking?"

He replied, "No."

"Ok then, what kind of drugs are you on? Acid? Meth? Coke? Medical?" I asked.

"No, not drugs, no drugs. This is how things go for me, this is the kind of thing that happens in my life."

"Then you're lucky that you're still alive." I said.

He replied, "I'm a good swimmer, a really good swimmer."

I thought, *no shit, or you'd be drowned*. The water temp is 68°F and the air temp is 52°F. I am thinking this man-fish probably has hypothermia and is semi-out of it.

"So where are your clothes, what's up with that?"

"I had to remove them once I fell in the lake. I took them off so I could swim."

That made sense, but maybe he could have kept the underwear.

Dave jumped into the discussion, "You parked at the public launch?"

"Yes, my truck is parked there."

"We are headed in and can drop you at your truck."

"No, my boat, we have to find my boat! My keys and wallet are in my boat. We have to find my boat! It went that way." Agitated, he pointed aggressively to the south.

Is it a good fish or bad man? What might he try to do? I thought. Then, I grabbed him by the back of his neck and pulled him face to face so I could look him directly in the eyes.

I said, "Calm down. You're in our boat. You're out of the water. You're safe now. Please calm down and relax."

As I looked into his eyes, I was thinking, *Good? or Bad?* Somehow, he read what I was thinking and responded, "I am not a bad guy. I just fell out of my boat."

This time we believed him, and we said, "OK, we'll take a look and see if we can find your boat. Just take it easy and sit down, relax. We'll help you."

"Dave, what's that light down there? Do see that light?"

Dave swung the boat around and said, "Let's go check it out."

About two miles down the shore line, we finally get to the light. It's a 21' Terra cruiser that had run aground. Somehow, it missed the rip rap & pilings. It had landed perfectly on a small sandy beach between two seawalls. Dave pulled the boat slowly into about 2' of water to let Fish-Man go.

"We release you...Go! Go get your boat." Dave said.

Fish-Man jumped out of the Lund and landed in the water. He looked happy to be free again and took off thru the water toward his beached boat. Then it occurred to me that he was headed for the *back* of the boat. The motor was engaged and prop was still turning.

"Dave, he is headed for the back of the boat, right at the prop."

Both Dave and I were yelling, "Not the back. Not the back! Go to the front! Holy sushi, he is headed right for the prop!"

Fish-Man disappeared under water and did not come back to the surface.

"Dave, I think he got into the prop."

Suddenly Fish-Man popped up at the shore line. He wiggled his way out of the water and stood up on the beach.

"Stay away from the back of your boat. The prop, we thought you were sushi. Now get in your boat and turn off the engine." We shouted.

Fish-man replied, "Aye-aye, Captain, right away, Captain."

He got in his boat and turned off the motor., saying, "It's all under control now, Captain. Your next orders, Captain… Sir?"

"Get out of the damn boat and see if you can push it free." Dave said.

"OK, Sir. Right away, Sir."

His boat was a beached whale, it did not budge.

"We'll give you a pull," Dave said as I threw him the anchor line to tie off to the back of his boat. A couple of tugs with the Lund and the beached whale was floating free, so Dave told him, "Now, follow us back to the pier."

Fish-Man was still totally naked. We thought he would have something in his boat to put on. Instead, he appeared to be engaged in an intense conversation with himself. We could hear him mumbling some justification for the night's adventure.

"I'm really a good guy. I just fell out of my boat. I'm a good swimmer, a really good swimmer."

His mumbled conversation continued and repeated several times as we slowly headed for the pier and up the Black River. I was not sure if Fish-Man was convincing himself or even believed his own shit!

"What do you think, Dave?" I asked.

"I think he's lucky. That boat could have a hole in it and be taking on water." Dave said.

I yelled to Fish-Man, "Turn on your bilge."

Fish-man turned on the bilge and only a small amount of water pumped out. His hull was apparently good.

Dave continued, "See, he's lucky: lucky that we didn't hit him and run him over with the Lund, lucky that he didn't drown, lucky that we caught him and pulled him into our boat, lucky that his boat ran safely ashore, lucky that it didn't go west toward Chicago. Lucky that he didn't end up in the propeller. Lucky that we helped him."

When we got upstream to the Idler, the bar was hopping. Fish-Man looked over at the bar and appeared to be thinking about stopping in for a drink and conversation. Yes, he was still naked.

"Just keep going, Dave. Let's leave him at the boat launch," I said.

When we arrived at the public launch, Fish-Man jumped on the dock and tied his boat off. Still totally naked, he walked off to get his truck.

"Let's go, Dave, it's too late for more fishing. Sometimes it's best to turn the big ones free, let them get away, or even cut the line." I said.

The next day we cleaned the perch at the River Bend Boat Club. Some friends stopped in the cleaning station and we told the story of the 260-270 pounder we had caught and released the night before. We went to our mom's place for a fish fry and bonfire. As family members arrived, we told the story again and again. The "Boat Loser," that lucky Fish-Man that we threw back for someone else to catch another day!

Meaning
DeMaris Gaunt

So tempting
to think rain
must mean
god is expressing
emotion,
sharing
in your epic
melancholy —
or the collision
between the semi
and the car
in front of you
means you were
favored
over the two children
who ended up
in the ER —
and the dead
towhee you almost
stepped on
must have been
placed on the trail
as a reminder
of how quick
and unfairly
all this might come
to an end —
and the
coneflower
must possess
all the magic
of the universe
because it leaves you
with the truth

after you pluck
its petals —
"he loves me"
which means
you can ignore
all the other signs
that say he doesn't.

Crazy Violin
Annie Oberman

Of Mice & Men
Sandra Stewart

Hangover

I woke up this morning with a stranger in my bed.
I should have known it would happen –
He was there when I went to sleep

The Last Time I Saw Bo

Bright shadow, dancing out of reach –
Touch down for a moment;
I will caress you.

Chinked armor, sheltering tender soul –
Fall open once more;
I will invade you.

Snake doctor, maybe lover,
There's fear in your electric eyes.
What can I do about it?
I only learned to breath last Sunday.

A Reminder

You don't need him to tell you, you can't
He doesn't need you to tell him he shouldn't
You don't need each other not to give love to
It's long past time to:
      Grow up, lonely children, and dance on your own four feet!

Hymn of Repentance

I invited you in, Miss Mousie
You were delighted to be so known
You brought all your friends, Miss Mousie
I killed them one by one

What beautiful trust you showed me
That beautiful trust I betrayed

My ignorance at times is unbounded
Forgive me for being afraid

You danced your joy around me
I saw only vermin and pests
I baited my trap for the slaughter
And closed my eyes to the rest

I beat the wounded to death with a hammer
But finally I did it with love
You understood then, Miss Mousie
And left, leaving only your blood

Confusion
Tim A. Baker

The alarm sounds, jolting me awake.

Confusion, yet with a familiar pain in my head. Then up for a shower, reviving and cleansing me. Rummaging mindlessly through shirts and ties. Looking for a match, but not caring. No appetite for breakfast. Just hot, black coffee.

Walking out the door, the rising sun reminding me my head hurts and I'm late for work. Pulling up to the office, wondering if this is really happening. Finally inside, short greetings and long stares exchanged. The work day moves forward, carrying me with it. I play the part, marveling at the seemingly endless charade.

Morning passes. Afternoon settles in. I remain unsettled, physically present but with my thoughts elsewhere. Thinking, longing, needing. My co-workers seemingly oblivious, or so I tell myself. Leaving work early, again. Some excuse, contrived. I think no one notices. Exit, stage nowhere. More stares.

Driving now, free and happy. But this road leads only to destruction. One stop. One drink. Then two. Then more. Talking, laughing, hiding, drinking. Then home, cautiously. Fumbling for keys in the lock. Stumbling inside. Dark. Cold. Alone. Time for another. Then another. Losing count, or not counting. Slipping away, not caring. Numb. Unable to move. Unwilling to try. Eyes closing.

The alarm sounds, jolting me awake.

Job Security
DeMaris Gaunt

Never mind
the fact that you
are in a position
of privilege
and have choices
to make about
where to dine
on Saturday night
and what kind
of hardwood
to use for your cabinets
in the new kitchen
you are able
to afford
and forget about
the sultry and exotic
places you'll travel to
in the spring
and in the winter—
you are about
to begin
the second half
of your life
bankrupt
with money to spare
but none of it
can buy back
that love you lost
while you were
too busy
accumulating
things you thought
would keep it.

Logan Street Flood, Run Bill Run!
Al Geisler

On the Floor

DeMaris Gaunt

The man
admires the woman
who is puckered up
posing
in a tight black dress
slit up the thigh
standing at a flattering angle
in what appears to be
a bathroom so public
the trash can is overflowing –
but the man doesn't care
about the brown
paper towels
and mascara stained tissues
on the floor
beside her 3 inch heel –
or that all of us can see her
insecurity
under that confident facade –
he is taken
by her red lips
and her youth
which makes him feel
she might
have a need for him
his wife no longer feels –
so he types
his approval
in just one word.
Wow.
No exclamation mark
to differentiate
his compliment
from his base desire

to crawl into that photo
and add her dress
to the pile on the floor.

Yordana
Radka Caviness

It is 1943 in Portland, Oregon. I am four years old and watching our landlady, Yordana Majovski (a tailor) and her husband Vasil Majovski (a carpenter) look at our backdoor, which doesn't close properly. They are fellow Macedonians and friends.

After a long inspection, Vasil tells my mother, "Yes, it needs to be fixed. I will remove the door and the doorjamb and this wall."

My mother looks dismayed and says, "Oh, I thought it would just be a simple repair."

To which Vasil says, "No, no, it needs to be done right. I will do this as a favor, when I can work it into my schedule."

The next morning, Yordana arrives with a piece of wood, a hammer, and some nails. I watch her hammer in the piece of wood; then she and my mother open and close the door.

My mother says, "It is perfect – thank you!"

Yordana says, "Luba, I do the quick fix."

Forever after, I admire and like Yordana immensely.

In Macedonia, Yordana married Vasil at sixteen (an arranged marriage) and she herself provided the means for the two of them and Vasil's younger brother Rade to leave Macedonia and come to America. Rade and his family live diagonally across the street from Vasil, Yordana, and their daughters Donna and Cathcrine, who are three and six years older than I am.

Yordana is the most capable Macedonian immigrant that we know. She easily speaks, reads, and writes English. I know Yordana owns: 1) many rental houses, and with Vasil's help, she divides each house into two rentals, and she is the rental manager; 2) a tailoring and alteration shop next door to her house; she is the tailor and seamstress; 3) *Podkrepa* (our Macedonian Social Club), in that, as secretary/treasurer, she organizes the business meetings, the Potluck Dinners, collects the membership dues, keeps the accounts. In 1950, under her leadership, *Podkrepa* proudly owns our own newly built meeting hall in north Portland.

Yordana also brought her brother Boris and his wife Keenche to America. They have a daughter Lilly (two years older than I am) and live directly across the street in one of Yordana's houses, in the upstairs rental.

In the summers, we often walk a mile east from our house to visit Yordana at hers. Her husband Vasil, their daughters Donna and Catherine, always are doing nothing. They wait for Yordana to come from her sewing shop and do the breakfast dishes while she makes lunch for them and us. Yordana always finds time to bring trays piled with *tatlia* (like Greek *baklava*) and meringue kisses and *Gourbidea* (Macedonian butter cookies) to weddings, funerals – any Macedonian gatherings. Her desserts are generous, welcomed treats.

Whenever I see Yordana at *Podkrepa*, at weddings, bridal and baby showers, in her tailoring shop, at her house or inspecting and repairing our backdoor – Yordana wears the same brown dress. I ask my mother why Yordana has only one dress?

My mother laughs and says, "She has a closet full of dresses; they are all alike. Yordana makes herself the same dress because she likes it so much."

Ten years later, in the same dress, with an orchid pinned at her shoulder, Yordana is the mother-of-the-bride at Donna's elegant downtown hotel ballroom wedding.

When we visit Yordana, I look out of the living room window and often Lilly is at her window and waves at me. I ask my mother, then run across the street, climb the stairs; Lilly is waiting for me. I like Lilly so much more than Donna and Catherine. At the kitchen table, we talk and color in her coloring books and play with her dolls. Lilly is sweet and quiet and pretty.

Lily's mother Keenche comes into the kitchen. She is beautiful; her face has a ready smile. She has coal-black hair; ruby lips, dancing dark eyes, and very tight-fitting clothes; tall strappy high-heeled shoes; dangling earrings, and bangle bracelets. Keenche is beautiful and welcoming; I like her very much.

Keenche tells us she is leaving, and that Lilly and I should help ourselves to a snack. Then, I hear Lilly's father Boris, who doesn't work (he drinks and gambles), yelling from the bedroom.

"Where are you going?"

She replies, "I am meeting a friend at the café."

Boris shouts, "Remember to show up tonight; if I don't win, you need to be there."

Keenche says, "Yeah, yeah, I'll be there," and then she says under her breath, "you always lose."

She winks at us and we watch her lovely figure disappear towards a nearby small shopping area.

Macedonians call female friends and foes "whore" when they are upset with them, but they call Keenche a "whore" when they are not mad at her at all, so I know she really is one.

In 1946, when I am seven, my family and Yordana's family go on a picnic together. My sister Olga is nine, my sister Ana is two. Yordana has recently had a son, Larry, who is four months old; Donna is thirteen and Catherine is ten. Their father Vasil has cancer and is very ill.

We drive to a rural wooded place and get out of our cars. My father rushes to Yordana's car. To our surprise he takes baby Larry in his arms. He carries Larry tenderly, lovingly; we all carry something for our picnic. We all pause at the edge of a steep wooded cliff; it has a narrow, rutted path to our picnic destination.

As we pause, Vasil, summoning an amazing strength, the strength of the dying, whirls upon my father and snatches Larry from him. Vasil's eyes are full of hate and loathing.

Vasil has given us a revelation; but there is nothing to be done. With Vasil leading the way, we climb the treacherous path to our strange sad picnic. Ten days later, Vasil dies.

It is still summer, but we no longer walk to Yordana's. The following year, my parents buy a house and we move to north Portland. We continue to see Yordana at *Podkrepa* social events.

It is 1987, I am forty-eight years old and visiting my mother in Portland, Oregon. I am there to see my maternal aunt Yetsa, who has come to Portland from Croatia and is nearing the end of her six-month visiting Visa. I am also there to attend my father's one-year-dead wake. Macedonians believe that an anniversary wake – the last celebration for a dead relative – is essential for the relative's bountiful life in the hereafter.

The afternoon of my father's anniversary wake, a car pulls into my mother's driveway. The car door opens – it is Yordana. She wears her brown dress. I see that it is a charming dress; simple, timeless, becoming, with a round neck, three-quarter sleeves, perfectly fitted bodice and hip line, and slightly flared to the hem. Yordana is opening her trunk and removing a wrapper from an enormous tray piled with Macedonian powdered-sugared-covered butter cookies.

She says, "Radka, I made these for your father, I wish I could have made more, but I ran out of time."

I tell Yordana they look wonderful; there is enough to feed an army. She smiles and says she cannot come in; she is on her way to work.

Yordana says, "Radka, you should be proud of me. At seventy, I went to school to get my certificate for practical nursing. It isn't easy to go to classes and take tests when you are seventy years old, but I did it! I am a Licensed Practical Nurse. I was doing it without a license, but the pay is less and you don't get the respect. I worked the night shift last night; midnight to 8:00AM and will again tonight, but I am filling in on the 4:00PM to midnight shift today as well. I will be there already at midnight so it won't be hard."

I am amazed and say she is incredible, and Yordana says, "I enjoy it, I am busy and needed."

I say, "You must have closed your tailoring shop."

And Yordana says, "No, I love my sewing and I have lots of clients who I make clothes for and do alterations for; I would never close my shop!"

I know she has greatly expanded her rental properties; I ask her how she can do all these things.

Yordana says, "Radka, I will tell you. I owe it all to my wicked stepmother. When I was six and my brother Boris was four, our mother died and our father remarried. She hated us and said I would be a slave and Boris, too. I had to do everything. I did the laundry, cooking, cleaning, made all of our clothes, everything she could think of for me to do. I resolved I would never let her or my father know how sad I was, how heartbroken; they would never see me cry. I pretended I liked the work and acted like she didn't have enough for me/us to do. I did Boris' work, too. Then a strange thing happened. I began to like it. People told my stepmother how lucky she was to have a stepdaughter like me. I needed more and more work. I began to make clothes and desserts for other people. I earned money from extra work. Soon my father and stepmother were dependent on *me*. My father began to adore me, he said there never could be another child like me. I gave my father money, I bought him several houses to rent so that he'd have income, and I saved money for myself to come to America. I promised myself, when I had children I would never have them do any work. Yes, I owe it all to my hateful stepmother."

Soon after Yordana told me this, I hear she bought three beachfront houses at Cannon Beach to add to her Portland rental empire. She paid $80,000 for each of them.

I know these houses. They sit side-by-side on the beachfront and are marvelous. On the top of the cliff was Persa and Andrew Jack's house – they are the richest Macedonians in Podkrepa and are Bertha's parents, the Bertha of my father's dreams. Next to it nestled half-way down the cliff was a huge log house and next to it, the third house, which was a large one-story at sand level. The road behind the houses dead-ends at the back of the cliff; there is a public easement access path between the log and one-story houses. I walked that path, as a child, countless times to the sand and the sea.

Twenty years after Yordana told her story, it is 2007, I am sixty-eight years old and live in Indiana. I talk to my sister Olga in Portland on the telephone each Saturday. Olga tells me that Yordana, now over ninety years old, regularly drives to the Oregon Coast to check on her beachfront rentals. She calls Olga, who is a recluse, to ask her to go with her to Cannon Beach. Olga always says no.

Yordana's Oregon Coast beachfront houses are worth over a million and a-half dollars each now. Yordana has the Midas Touch; she turns her work to gold.

Footnote added by Jim Caviness, Sr. ("Small World – from my point of view"):

MY DESTINY
If I had had the gypsy power of seeing the future:

In 1956, I'm selling men's clothes at Meier & Frank's (Oregon's largest department store), and I work with a temp named Catherine Majovski.

We couldn't have known then that two years later, I would marry a woman I had not yet met; Catherine's half-brother's half-sister (Larry and Radka, respectively).

A Tale of Two Cities
Sandra Stewart

Love Letter to Boston (1980)

I borrowed that title, but then;
A lady like Boston gets a lot of love letters.
Here's one more:
     You assaulted me when I walked outside today –
     Assaulted me with your magnificence.
     Reaching toward me from every direction.
     Little beckoning leaf tips,
Acres of convoluted fairy castle roof tops,
Flute music!
Oz across the Charles.
Your air aswarm with vibrant, delicately stated loveliness!
Dear lady, God blessed us well with you.

Ode on Noblesville (1983)

Thank you for embracing your stray again –
Wiser, older, sweeter, softer
Having chased her rainbows, now finds them
Floating placidly above your homely streets.

As plain as old shoes, you are –
Comforting and welcoming.
Here I feel complete, at home.
Not known, of course;
But valued.

The Way Through
Kristina Oliver

The Emperor's New Clothes are Made in China (A Fake Fairy Tale)

Sandra Stewart

The Swamp King was disgruntled, miffed and really, really ugly. His ugliness did not personally distress him, for he thought himself beautiful; but the reflection he saw in other eyes absolutely enraged him! He wanted ALL the creatures – in and out of the swamp – to see him as the brilliant, beautiful, and powerful king he knew himself to be. He didn't care to *be* brilliant or beautiful, just to be viewed so by *all* others. If only he had hands, he could make them kiss his ring.

His tiny, shriveled soul still technically belonged to him, but he had no real use for it. He was perfectly willing to sell it to the highest bidder, if bidders there were. Hearing none, he would consider trading it for his damaged heart's desiring – to be looked at and adored, or at least respected. Feared would be even better. But, there were no bidders in the murky swamp – no customers for that which he wished to sell. In fact, he could no longer give it away! The slimy, smelly, squishy swamp had grown too small for him. Though he still felt comfy in the familiar embrace of its sticky depths, he longed to soar aloft like the vultures wheeling overhead in search of carrion.

The day the Wandering Wizard tumbled through the vile miasma and into the swamp was the beginning of the petulant King's ridiculous dream of glory. The Swamp King could become the Emperor of the Earth with a bit of magic, transmogrification, prestidigitation and flat out flim-flam perpetrated by the rapidly putrefying wizard! Such was his panic that the Wallowing Wizard made a *very, very* bad deal in exchange for his freedom. All the Finally Freed Wizard received was a damaged, withered soul and a few filthy rubles – a very bad deal for himself and for *all* creatures other than the Swamp King and his cohorts. For the Desperate Wizard contrived a most peculiar spell – custom designed for the viciously needy Swamp King. Mr. Wizard did not turn the hideous Swamp King into a handsome prince, but rather disguised him as a mirror that mesmerized and compelled Desperate Seekers to tumble through in search of solutions to sadness and want. There was Kool-Aid through the looking glass! Some Seekers took only a tiny sip, which they spat on the ground immediately upon tasting its foul bitterness. Others swallowed it down, choking and grimacing. (They didn't really like it, but were willing to try to develop a taste since they WERE thirsty and saw no alternative down the rabbit hole.) Sad!

Alas, too many found it effortless to imagine the Kool-Aid as nectar of the gods, life-saving medicine – or at the very least, Ensure. Few even noticed the faint smell of Hemlock on the rim of their glass. They found, instead, the precise flavor they most craved. They saw and tasted the answer to their prayers; the lid to their kettle; the awakening from their nightmare! They arose, lauded and followed THE ONE who could deliver their salvation. They guzzled the nectar, and sated; they believed.

You may be thinking that this peculiar spell was a harmless bit of tomfoolery. It was not. It most definitely was not. The Seekers, having found the apparently perfect panacea for their pain – the fulfillment of their hearts desiring – stopped seeking and became tangled up in believing that the looking glass contained all that they required. The acclaim from the believing, adoring, enraptured Kool-Aid Drinkers emboldened the warty, malformed Swamp King to crawl from the mire, *attempt* to walk erect, and seize the Golden Crown of Accomplishment! After surprising himself (and devastating the Still Thirsty) by securing the crown, he lost no time before proceeding to pummel and trample the Earth over which he now believed himself to rule. And the Earth wept. Very, very Sad!

What a revolting development, the Still-Thirsty, Un-mesmerized Creatures cried with ONE VOICE! Alas for the new Emperor, the Earth was still abloom with beauty and replete with creatures of discriminating taste who ignored the Looking Glass, avoided the Hemlock and continued to look at and through him. They clearly saw a repugnant, vapid Swamp Creature with a shriveled soul instead of a dazzlingly magnificent Emperor. "Not my Emperor!" they cried. This truly, deeply, enraged the Emperor, *neé* King, and further fueled his pain. Disaster!

Furious and frustrated by their resistance (and not given to introspection) the newly minted Emperor sought solace by causing pain to others. He lashed out at any who challenged, criticized, or just plain failed to adore him. He hurt them by hurting their mother, the Earth, and by taking away that which they most needed to thrive – or survive. Their rights became most uncivil. But still, they failed to adore him. Still they resisted and fought; still they ratted him out and thwarted his twisted ambition at every opportunity. Oh, the Earth most assuredly trembled in his wake, which was somewhat satisfying though just a bit scary because, after all, he now dwelt on terra firma. But still, he pined for more, and more and more. Sick!

To those awash in plenty, he gave plenty more. Those who showered him with plenty and praise, he heaped with glory and anointed with power over the Plentiless. The chosen Bad & Plenty wallowed in their plunder like sows in mud; pigs in shit (unless they crossed him).

When their posh pens became too restrictive, they rutted, bit and devoured – all, like the Emperor, seeking that which continued to elude them. To those who failed to be bamboozled by their bombast, they cried "liar, liar pants on fire!" To those who failed to laud and adore them, they cried "So's your old man!" , and "You are, but what am I?" Without enough of the privilege, respect, fear and adoration they craved and considered their due, they too became increasingly more dangerous, running amuck and grabbing all that was cherished by the Plentiless. Eventually, they morphed from hogs and pigs into rats and stool pigeons. Chaos!

But the most dangerous and unpredictable of all the Bad & Plenty was the Emperor of the Earth. Would he destroy everything in his wake, or take his ball and go home? Would he find enlightenment and alter his awful ways? Would he have a snit fit and destroy the world? Or, would the Un-Mesmerized Creatures with ONE VOICE expose his seamy underbelly, deport him to the swamp, and reign triumphant just in the nick of time?

To be continued (hopefully), but
Frighteningly near THE END

New Year
DeMaris Gaunt

DeMaris 2018

Home Invasion

Nicole Amsler

Tie for *Third Place*, Prose Category

The day had been long and was about to get longer. Deselection day at the library required the locating, untagging, and disposing of unimportant books and Jennie smelled of book paste, dust, and ancient ink. She yearned for a long soak in their claw foot tub and an hour alone with one of the books saved from the purge.

Instead, they were hosting a coterie of young marrieds from their church, at Byron's exuberant invitation. The thought of invading guests and an evening of forced oversharing settled a mantle of dread across her shoulders. She felt as if the weight might press her into the mud of the driveway. If the evening plans only included time alone with Byron, she would be as light as a dust mote.

Delayed by the deselection, she didn't have time for a shower before tackling the evening's *hors d'oeuvres*. She cubed cheese while mini sausages burbled in her new crock pot, fat and noisy in their barbeque bath. Jennie used the last of the ground coffee and sugar, sighing at the week-old grocery list she had posted on Byron's side of the refrigerator. She spilled out deformed lumps of pickles and, as an afterthought, speared each one with a fancy frilled toothpick, imagining each one as a poor man's voodoo doll.

Give them all a headache or maybe a pulled hamstring. Perhaps a 24-hour bug. *Nothing serious*, she thought, as she stabbed each one. Just something to prevent all the guests from raiding her living room.

Over the cool tang of the vinegar and pickle juice, she smelled burning tires. Peeking out through kitchen's corner window, she expected Byron's truck and felt the first smile of the day ease her face. She only saw the empty, muddied circular driveway, a half parenthesis at the base of their farmhouse. Her shoulders wilted in disappointment as she returned to filling the cheese tray.

Jennie flipped on the light switch to the dining room with her elbow, hefting a bulky tray of generic club crackers and cheese squares. Her scream reverberated through the room, echoed by the crashing platter and skitter of crackers.

The adjacent room was alive with tiny orangey-red beetles. Masses pooled in corners, like blackened blood. They traversed from window sills out along the room's walls, in thick tendrils. Clusters hugged armchair bends, air registers, and sconces. Individual ladybugs peppered the floors and walls, creating a montage of writhing, terrifying life.

She crept across the open room to inspect a cluster, their shells crunching like gravel under her shoes. Each ladybug fluttered its fingernail shiny wings in a ballet of random movements. They did not pile up, like boisterous children, but rather spread like poorly aligned mosaic tiles.

She pinched one between her fingernails and studied it.

The screen door slammed.

"Lock up your valuables, I'm home!" Byron's usual greeting had been funny the first time and normally she smiled. Today she was both frazzled and irritated.

She crunched back across the floor, ballet leaping across the ruined cheese cubes, several now dotted with a ladybug topper, like tiny petit fours. Byron stood at the fridge, door open, milk jug at his lips.

"Don't drink that. We don't have any cream for the coffee. I was going to use the milk."

"Too late," he said, slamming the empty jug on his hip, crumpling it. He pitched it toward the lidded garbage bin but missed. Jennie bent and retrieved it.

"We have a problem," she said. He slid over and draped his arms around her, his sleeves still sprinkled with sawdust. He tried to nuzzle her neck as relief flooded her. He would cancel and they would be alone tonight but first he needed to see.

"We have a ladybug infestation," she said. "You have to cancel tonight."

"Fear not, little lady," he said, dipping her, his rough hand at the back of her neck. "I'll kill the big, bad bugs for you. I think the task might even be listed in our wedding vows. Love, honor, cherish, and kill bugs."

He always got giddy when a party was on his horizon. Meanwhile, she felt stiff and trapped in a room of people. Either way, tonight's party wasn't going to be in her house.

"Please, just go look." She shrugged out of his arms.

"Fine, I'll go," he said. He shot her a smile, white milk still filmed across his teeth before dashing off to the next room.

She heard the crunch before she heard his curse.

"What the hell!"

Relieved, she entered the room and watched him study the clusters and check the seals on the old farmhouse windows. He joined her, properly frazzled. It would be them against the infestation, a battle to be chuckled over on their 25th anniversary.

"You have to cancel," she said. "Do you need their phone numbers or are they in your phone? We can't have people over when…" She couldn't even finish the statement, the enormity of the mess multiplying in her mind and at her feet. Thank goodness they weren't spiders but there was a whiff of filth about them, prissed up with orangey paint.

"Ladybugs are lucky," he said, prodding a mass. "But this borders on ridiculous. Do you smell that?" Byron tilted his head back, exposing the gaping holes of his nostrils at Jennie, mouth parted. She averted her eyes, just as she did when he used the toilet in front of her, the violent stream of urine terrifying her with its strength. She was mortified to think he might find some habit of hers as odious as she considered his baser instincts. The lack of privacy in marriage was startling.

She sniffed as well, nose lowered, mouth closed. It still smelled like burning tires.

"Hot tar!"

Jennie knelt to gather the ruined cheese and Byron nearly bowled her over, exiting the room. Seconds later, she heard the click of his computer keys, further alleviating the heaviness and anxiety which had been perched on her shoulders ever since he volunteered their house. As he cancelled, she could begin the steady task of eradicating the infestation.

She lost the sound of his tip-tacking on the computer keys when she ran the canister vacuum. A whirlwind of ladybugs created a blender effect in the see-through canister. She started by kneeling in front of the garage-sale ivory brocade chairs, relocated just last night into the plagued room. Tiny dots of urine yellow appeared where the bugs had once been. She licked her finger and scrubbed at a mark, which spread.

Knees pebbled in dead bugs, she rose and vacuumed the windowsills. It was in her nature to attack a job methodically. Dishes were washed in the proper order: glassware, china, silverware, pots and pans. Meals were eaten clockwise on the plate, protein, vegetable, bread, fruit. Her first dinner with her in-laws had launched her into a quandary. The apple salad was drowned in thinned mayonnaise, dotted with half moons of celery, sunflower seeds, slivers of fatty bacon, and grape halves. She left the salad untouched, unable to categorize it.

She worked in one-foot squares, clearing the crowded clusters, leaving the strays for last. She was beginning to see conquered space, a glimpse at victory.

She was in the midst of clearing the window ledge when the vacuum died.

"Stop," Byron said, taking the nozzle from her and letting it clatter to the floor, spewing pardoned bugs across a once cleared section. He said, "You're making it worse."

"How?" she asked, arms crossed, protective.

"The bugs excrete a tiny portion of their blood when frightened. See there in the vacuum cleaner? It's their blood and it smells like tar. It's the same pheromone that tells them it's safe to winter here... No, that can't be right..." He picked up a single bug and scrutinized it closely, as if directions were written on its black belly.

"No matter, they still need to go. They can't stay," she said, an edge of panic in her voice. She wouldn't cohabitate with a swarm of beetles, even if they were painted with whimsical polka dots.

"We'd have to remove the walls and the studs and… then we'd have to replace every stained spot in the house, just to try to get rid of them. We're just going to have to live with the bugs every fall. They're in it for the long haul." Bryon said.

"I refuse to believe that. Did you get reach everyone? To cancel." She watched a clean swath become peppered with meandering bugs.

"No, I'm sure everyone will be fine with it. In fact, I can ask them if they have any advice." He didn't meet her eyes but he hugged her, aiming for her neck and she slammed her head to her shoulder, blocking him and banging them both. Her teeth rattled.

"You actually expect me to welcome six people into our house when the place is infested?" she asked, furious at him and the waste of time. He could have been helping her clean. He could have understood.

"It's not the whole house," Byron said. "It's only a room. One room."

They argued a little while longer, in newly worn ruts, already too steep to escape. He said she was being irrational, inflexible. He said she looked for any excuse to cancel. She said he was selfish, pigheaded, more concerned with a party than her feelings. They had squabbled before but this was betrayal.

Still there was comfort in the way the fight progressed on its familiar path. She could almost time his departure out the back door to get a tool which would solve the whole problem. If she ventured out to the tilted pole barn behind him, she knew she'd find him playing on his phone, that game with the infernal beeping and jackpot sounds. But she didn't follow.

Alone in the house once more, she abandoned the bugs, and climbed the stairs to lie on their bed. He'd be gone for at least twenty minutes, too late to call the guests. Too late to choose her.

Their bedroom was lit by the evening's dusk. The single window in the room faced south, just as the room below did but there were no ladybugs. A rosy glow permeated the room. It was both a sad light and a warm light.

"Marriage takes work," her mother had said, straightening Jennie's veil. It was one of the many platitudes she had heard in church, from friends, from family, and in trite little gift books people gave brides-to-be.

Of course, it takes work, Jennie thought. Just as preparing dinner according to a recipe or filing books according to the Dewey decimal system was considered work. You followed the prescribed plan and in the end, you had a finished product.

But as it turned out, marriage was grunt work. It was the exhausting work of hauling and cataloging books from their shelves to another, only to reverse the process the next week. It was the tedious work of picking pine needles out of Berber carpet after the holiday season.

Marriage was the infestation of orange beetles, accumulating until they could not be ignored, excreting their trademark scent of terror and *amour*, beckoning to more dysfunctional lovers.

Jennie heard the clank of a pan on the stove downstairs. The light was dying, marking the inevitable. She debated hiding upstairs, leaving Byron to play host. Her claw-footed tub and book called to her. Listening to Byron sing to the radio, off-key and warbling, she pictured him not as her hero but as her flotation device, buoyant and life-saving. She slid off the bed and walked downstairs, her anger evaporating a degree with each step.

Byron had thumb-tacked a king size sheet across the doorway to the shameful room, its cheery floral pattern belying the swarm behind it. In the kitchen, Byron flipped mini pancakes dotted with chocolate chips, the only food left in the house, an odd choice to feed guests but what were their options?

"Hey, sweetness. See what I made?" he said, his voice full of boyish glee. "Ladybug pancakes. What a story to tell. We can offer tours."

He winked at her. The room filled with light as the first car pulled in, swinging its headlights across her kitchen cupboards, illuminating every flaw equally: the chipped porcelain handle on one door, the grease splatters that never came clean, Byron's favorite coffee cup with half of the paint wore off, and the wedding present of a clock, always five minutes off.

Byron handed her the spatula, still warm from his hand. He pecked her on the cheek and rushed to swing open the door.

"Welcome to the house of horrors," he said to the couple ascending the steps. "Man, do we have a story for you."

As they entered, a single ladybug strolled across the counter, edging toward the small plate of pancakes. Jennie discreetly placed Byron's coffee cup over the bug and then turned to smile, in terror, in *amour*.

The Care Giver

Lorraine Rosio

A woman is more likely to provide family care
A woman is more likely to experience depression
A woman, a family care giver, is more likely to live in poverty
A woman, a family care giver, is more likely to receive government
assistance

This is my life
This is who I am

However misunderstood
However frustrating
However joyless
However reclusive
However sad
There exists in me an intense need to help

Is this my life's calling
Is this my journey to be accepted
While caring for others have I also been taking care of myself

Is there a return
Should a return be expected
Is this a selfless act
I care
I need
I want
But can you give
Do you give

The Smoking and Joking Santa

Mark Wilkinson

Tie for *Third Place*, Prose Category

When you're a kid, the whole concept of Santa is a test. The slow metamorphosis from willing believer through quiet doubter to avid debunker is a road that we all travel. Along the way, we have certain moments that create the suspicions that finally force us, as naive children, to accept the fact that our family, as well as society as a whole, has been playing what can only be described as a cruel joke on its most vulnerable citizens.

Of course, most kids have the lights come on as a series of small events occur. They see multiple Santas at the mall. They realize that reindeer cannot fly. They find presents in the closet. Santa's handwriting is identical to mom's. Nobody can drink that many glasses of milk and eat that many cookies in one night. One plus one equals two. The thin veneer peels off, and the joy of Christmas becomes the joy of being in the know. These are the common and time-honored ways of disabusing children from their belief in Santa Claus.

There are, of course, other, less traditional methods.

I was beginning to become the quiet doubter, but had not yet taken the plunge to cynicism. Then Santa showed up one Christmas Eve. One of the problems with parenting during the "Santa is real" part of a kid's life is knowing just when to pull the plug. Or at least knowing when to bring up the "Santa's helpers" concept. Sadly, my parents were not ready to introduce that concept when Santa made his visit.

On Christmas Eve one year, Santa and my older brother Gary came in the back door. Santa was loud. He was impeccably attired with a red bag over his shoulder. He was, as I heard my mom say later, "three sheets to the wind," a sailing metaphor with which I was unfamiliar.

Santa sat down at the kitchen table, lit a cigarette, and called me over. He pulled out the largest candy cane I had ever seen from his bag and presented it to me with a flourish, asking if I had been good. Glancing at my parents, I told him I had.

This obvious lie is another of the problems with the ruse of Santa. Kids are told that Santa knows if they are being bad. Parents use this cudgel to demand and enforce obedience throughout the year. But kids *are* bad. We lie, steal, dodge, and generally act in the most dishonorable ways possible. We *know* we are bad. But we lie to Santa Claus and he *believes* us. And our parents believe us. Even though we know it is bad, we learn that lying works.

So I lied to Santa while he was sitting at our kitchen table smoking. He smiled at me and told me to get good grades and brush my teeth. I watched in confusion as my parents spoke to Santa like they knew him. Then my brother took a bottle of Calvert's whiskey from the cabinet, a bottle of Coke from the Frigidaire, and poured both himself and Santa something called a highball. They all sat and laughed while I, ignored by them, gnawed on the monstrous candy cane. My eyebrows furrowed and my eyes narrowed as I worked out fact from fiction.

Santa stayed for an hour or so, still acting jolly. In fact, he got jollier. He smoked, joked, and drank highballs. Normally, Santa being in the house on Christmas Eve and believing my blatant lies about being good would be cause for celebration, but something felt different. I didn't yet know the word *conspiracy*, but something did not seem right. Who was this Santa Claus? I decided to investigate.

I knew my mom and dad wouldn't tell me anything. They never did. I reached my own conclusions, often on dubious evidence. My brother would tell me, though. Our relationship was different. Gary was 17 years older than I, more of a visitor in my life than a constant presence. He normally was generous with me. He gave me rides in his sports car, bought me a BB gun and a science kit, and introduced me to Little Annie Fanny in *Playboy* when I was a pre-teen. All of that was in the future. At this time, he was home from the Marines and was spending a lot of time at the local bars in town.
I caught him a few days later and asked him about Santa's behavior at our house. Gary, in the process of making a bologna and potato chip sandwich, gave me a long look and asked me what I thought.

"I didn't think Santa smoked cigarettes," I said.

Gary looked at me.

"And I didn't think he drank highballs."

Gary continued to look at me.

"And he cussed."

Gary smiled and said, "So, what do you think?"

"I don't think that was Santa, but everybody acted like he was. I think everybody was lying to me."

"Is that all?" he said.

"No," I said. "I don't think Santa's real anymore. Who was that on Christmas Eve?"

"That was my friend Ben," he said. "He came into the bar handing out candy canes. I brought him home to give you one."

"Why did everyone lie to me?"

"Do you like the presents?" Gary said as he spread Miracle Whip onto his sandwich.

"Yeah," I said.

"So why do you care if everyone lied to you? Act like you believe the lie, and lie right back to 'em."

"It doesn't seem right to me," I said.

"So what? Take the presents. Merry Christmas."

He gave me half of his bologna and potato chip sandwich and sat down at the table. I sat down next him, took a crunchy bite, and thought about this new perspective. Lying was good.

This could change everything.

I Hear God's Voice

Reina DeCapua

I hear God's voice in the song of a bird
Knowing you're near without saying a word
I hear God's voice in the song of a bird
Talking to me without saying a word

The winter days are cold dark and gray
Like how my soul feels I try to pray
You comfort me as much as you can
How you comfort me, you comfort me

I hear God's voice in the song of a bird
Knowing you're near without saying a word
I hear God's voice in the song of a bird
Talking to me without saying a word

Early one morn I wake up and hear
Nature's noises, filling my ears
Each bird in harmony singing a song
It fills my soul, it fills my soul

I hear God's voice in the song of a bird
Knowing you're near without saying a word
I hear God's voice in the song of a bird
Talking to me without saying a word

Blood Brothers

Jerry Dreesen
Second Place, Prose Category

In the valley autumn had begun its cycle of dying. The winding path leading to the cabin ahead was strewn with early leaves, yellow ash silvered with rain that misted mid-air all afternoon. The cabin was small and worn, gray as sorrow, a thin string of smoke from the chimney rose then disappeared as though never there.

"Anybody home?" I called, knocking on the door. The door opened slightly.

"What do you want?"

"Looking for John Foster. You him?"

"Might be. Might not. Who are you? Tell me quick. Can't keep the door open forever."

"I'm from the Sheriff's office. You know Billy Hastings?"

The door gave way to a wider opening. A tall man with large hands filled the door frame. "I know him. I know Billy. Knowed him all my life. Best friends, me and Billy."

He stepped back and motioned for me to come inside.

The cabin was warm, filled with amber glow from two kerosene lamps. One on the table in the middle of the room, the other next to an old bentwood rocker. The floor was covered partly by a braided rug worn smooth from years of being there.

Neither of us spoke for a time, mesmerized, perhaps, by the fire, the slow heartbeat of the grandfather clock.

"I've knowed Billy my whole life," the man repeated. "Since we were kids. Growed up together, gettin' into all kinds of scrapes and fights. When we where twelve ... well, he was twelve, I was close to bein', we took a blood oath, pricked our thumbs and held them together, his and mine, so our bleeding'd touch and we'd be blood brothers for all time and circumstance. We always tell each other everything, you know. The good and the not so. Things said that make each other laugh or words that suffer serious thinkin'. We're like that, you know – brothers."

He looked at his hands – weathered and veined like the ash leaves lying on the graveled path.

"Why you here, Sheriff? Why you lookin' for Billy?"

"Well, not really looking." I said, "I've come with sorry news, John. Billy's dead. The Tolbert boys found him hanging from a tree in their ravine, note pinned to his breast pocket. He had written your name, gave instructions to come tell you."

Big John Foster sat in front of the fire for a long time leaning toward it, staring at his hands, running his finger across his thumb.

"You see? Damn fool! That's just like Billy. Course he wants me to know! He's my best friend, ol' Billy. He always tells me everything."

Talkin' Indiana

Jean Roberts
(song lyric)

Welcome to Indiana, the place I call my home
A lotta states got some little things funny and in Indiana I got me some
So stick with me while I sing my song, it's just a few verses so it won't take long
Talkin' about Indiana, the place I call my home

Driving in Indiana, hurry thru that yellow light
 You might not be in such a hurry tonight – but the guy behind you in the truck just might
So slide on thru, watch 'em follow you, they got people to see, they got business to do
Drivin' in in Indiana, drive on thru that yellow light

Saturday in Indiana! Meet your friends at the liquor store
You can't buy booze on Sunday – so if you'll want it then, y' gotta buy a little more
On Saturday in Indiana, and that's what this verse is for
So on Saturday in Indiana – Meet your friends at the liquor store

The farmer in Indiana, he's not just a pretty face
He's gotta know how to run his show or he'd end up losing the old home place
He drives his tractor to and fro, he's gonna plant his crop, he's gonna make it grow
The farmer in Indiana, he's not just a pretty face

The politician in Indiana, if you look on the other hand
Has gotta be pretty – gotta talk well – gotta be something like a country ham
He's got the gift of gab and that ain't all – he's got some other friends waitin' out in the hall
Politics in Indiana – it is the finest in the land!

The farmer met the politician down at the local liquor store

He said "I don't know what you done for me – but I do know what you done me for
You won the vote and then you left the state; they gave your seat to your nameless mate"
The farmer and the politician, at the local liquor store

Summer in Indiana! How to get from there to here?
You can't go east and you can't go west – y' got constructions zones from far to near
You can't go north and you can't go south, it makes me want to run my mouth
Summer in Indiana – you can't get from there to here!

So if you come to Indiana, drive on thru that yellow light
Go to the liquor store on Saturday and thank the farmer on a Saturday night
Enjoy the politics and the dirty tricks, watch road construction for special kicks,
Welcome to Indiana and y'all come back some time!

Holy Ghost
Gail Mehlan

May 20, 2016. Tonight is the CD release party for my youngest son's band, *Fur Coats for Sportsmen*, at a bar called "Hattrix" in Kenosha, Wisconsin. This is a big deal for them as this is their first "real" album and this is the first day that it will be available for purchase in stores or on iTunes. There had been some very positive press releases about their CD and their band, prior to the show. Even though we have had some ups and downs in the past, we want to show our son that we care deeply about what is happening in his life and will be there tonight to support him.

We walk out of the rain into the bar, not knowing what to expect here. It is a dark and dreary night, for sure. We'd been told that the show would start at 9:30, but nothing was happening yet. I step up to the bar.

"Bud Light or PBR?"

"PBR, thanks!"

I grab a beer and head toward the stage. Half-interested eyes glare at us with slight suspicion as we walk through what appears to be a replica of a cavern. It is dark in here and there are little areas to each side that look like caves. We don't look like typical customers here.

I am wearing a bright orange sundress and a cute jean jacket with beige sandals. I am a bright spotlight in a sea of black, black stockings, black leather jackets, black hair with streaks of purple, well worn Doc Martin boots, a few tattoos and piercings and something with a chain. My husband stays close as he walks cautiously beside me, guiding me. I suspect he feels a bit protective. His silver hair shines brightly under the decorative lights as we pass. No "skeletons" are tattooed to his arm or embroidered onto his shirt. I assume I'm not the only one experiencing this uncomfortable sensation, I'm sure he feels it, too.

The air is fragrant with stale beer and the fog from the vaping patrons. Each whiff reminds me of smoked cherry, actually pleasant. Dark corners erupt with laughter as we pass. I'm sure we look like lost souls. To come here was definitely out of our comfort zone, but we are here to support someone special tonight.

Suddenly, above the chatter of the crowd I hear,

"Hey, Mom!"

I am immediately enveloped in strong arms. The. Best. Hug. Ever. We linger there for a moment, both of us…comforted…welcomed.

"I'm so glad you came tonight!"

"Me, too! I'm excited to hear you play!

"Yeah…we should be starting here in a few minutes! We're waiting for more people to show up!"

"Did you get your CD?"

"No! They didn't give me one."

"I'll go get one for you…." My son replies, turning around and walking back into a dark corner.

We hadn't been up to see one of his shows for a long time. This is not where his father and I usually "hang out", and it's a very long drive for us. We had recently moved to central Indiana so we were thrilled to have this opportunity. Before the show we were able to spend a little bit of time with our son's fiancé and grabbed a bite to eat with her. In a few short weeks, we will welcome grandchild number five to the family. She isn't sure how long she would last tonight and we understand. She decides to go on home and we went on to the bar without her. We so enjoyed our brief visit with her, she's upbeat and seems happy, even though she's uncomfortably pregnant.

So…we wait…trying to relax…for the music to start. Several people come up to us and introduce themselves. A young man with a plaid shirt with sleeves rolled up to show off his "inked" arms, approaches and says,

"Hey…are you Mike's parents?"

"Yes, we are…"

"I'm one of Mike's customers at the bar, at Ron's Place. He's such a great guy. Always kind…always friendly. He's so smart…and so talented…I'm waiting for him to give me private guitar lessons!"

"Ok, great…" I stammer, "So nice to meet you!"

And then someone else (a young girl, pink hair, lip ring, black on black) overhears us.

"Oh my gosh…. YOU'RE Mike's mom? I love Mike…I work with him at the bar. He's a great guy! You've been awesome parents. So glad you could come tonight!"

"Thanks!" I smile, "Nice to meet you, too!"

I'm suddenly floating up into the vapor surrounding me to a place of pride and happiness…

He's a great guy… I think to myself… A great guy.

You see, it wasn't that long ago that I felt like I was a failure at the whole parenting thing. We had so many battles with our son over school, his behavior, his choices and the consequences. He was always a bit of a "rebel" and fought us on just about everything.

Then there was the drug addiction and the recovery and the relapses and the separation of our lives. There were hard decisions. We had to let him work out his life on his own terms. I, we, his father and I…never gave up completely, though. We prayed for him constantly and tried everything in our power to straighten him out. By our standards it didn't seem to happen. We finally let him be…his own person, in his own way. Now, he's living his life and finding his strength to do so on his own. As I sip my beer and wait, I'm lost in my thoughts about how he'll soon be a dad…so hard to believe!

Then the music starts and I'm awash in the sounds and the lights. The energy of the crowd is contagious. They move in close and sway and sing along as the band plays their music, familiar to those there, but loud and harsh to my unaccustomed ears. It seems an electrical charge ignites the crowd as the band plays all of their "Fur Coats" favorites. Dancing, moving bodies are waves undulating as the sounds crash against my eardrums.

Between songs:

"Hey…I'd like to give a shout out to my parents who came all the way from Indiana tonight to hear us play! Thanks so much for coming to support us!"

Loud cheers, screams, and whistles as interested faces turn and grin at us…with a warm welcome. Who would have thought? Again, I am elevated to a level of pride and appreciation that has been a long time coming…long past the expectation of it.

Suddenly I hear in the midst of a very "heavy" metal rock and roll song, the words,

"Holy Ghost…Holy Ghost…"

And I think I'm hearing wrong, but, no… Again…

"Holy Ghost,
Holy Ghost, Holy Ghost
Tell me what you know

Holy Ghost, Holy Ghost
What do you know?
What you know
What you know 'bout me?

And if you didn't know
You're 'bout to know 'bout me
Yeah, if you didn't know,
You're 'bout to know 'bout me" [1]

I'm not sure at the moment what this means. I begin to experience my own sort of Pentecost here. I feel awash with emotion as if the spirit itself has descended into this place. It has touched me here. This place that would to the "judgmental me" have been more like "hell" than a place to receive the spirit…but it is here that I do. I experience it. It is a blanket of reassurance covering my doubts with comfort and warmth. The spirit is

---

[1] "Holy Ghost" written by Justin Minch and Michael Mohr Maulin' Mehlan from the CD, *Loud Noises.* Recorded by Fur Coats Collective LLC 2016

here just as much if not more than it would be in a sterile church. This is where the spirit finds those it needs to touch, including me. And indeed, I have been touched. I'm "*'bout to learn 'bout*" my son!

In the quiet after the music stops, as my ears are ringing and my heart is full of love and respect, my doubts diminish. Another young woman, with a splash of purple hair and skeletons on her stockings, comes forward and introduces herself to me…

"Hello, my name's Katie… and I just want you to know that your son has been such a good friend to me. I love his music…he's a good man. He's gonna be an awesome dad."

My heart soars and almost bursts with love and pride…

"I'm Gail, thank you, so nice to meet you!"

And I think, but don't say it…

Yes, we have raised a good man, a good, kind, gentle, generous, talented man.

Damages
DeMaris Gaunt

Back at home
there are two
pencil drawings
precious
small
old
black and white
sketches
a gift from a friend
who means
something to me
but I can't decide
what
kind of frame
would be best
and I'm standing
in the aisle
deciding
whether my choices
are as black and white
as these frames
so I take my time
make a decision
proceed
to the checkout
where the cashier
is careless
and scratches
one of the corners
says to me
all you need to do
is touch that up
with some black paint
and I say
you know that dent
is never
coming out

BREAKING NEWS!
Alys Caviness-Gober

BREAKING NEWS!
Local Archaeologist Unearths Lost Wall
(Source: *FegenKurzmeldung*)

As a stroke-survivor, local archaeologist Alys Caviness-Gober rediscovers treasures long forgotten (by her) several times a day, but today's rediscovery of a Lost Wall is significant because it puts to rest a decades-long torrid debate between herself and her husband, former-maritime-archaeologist Cris Gober. Gober's theory has long been that the Lost Wall disappeared into a nefarious multi-dimensional space/time vortex much like the Bermuda Triangle or the Lost City of Atlantis.

"Damn wall just disappeared overnight years ago. There's a 'Lost City' somewhere at the bottom of some ocean, right? So why not a 'Lost Wall' right here in Noblesville?" argues Gober, with his usual infallible logic.

His wife, however, dismisses her husband's theory with a roll of her eyes and snort of derision, "Whatever!" she says with scientific certainty. "He can say that all he wants, but the fact is that a Lost Wall was right here all along, and my rediscovery today proves it."

Caviness-Gober told this reporter that her excavation of a Lost Wall occurred quite accidentally, while she was excavating a culturally significant section of a portion of an internal upper level area of a residential structure in Noblesville. The work in today's section is part of a larger project; the stratigraphic excavation, cataloguing, and removal of twenty-plus years worth of culturally significant goods in the residential structure of what appears to be a small group belonging to a clan whose lineage and members may be traced to similar peoples in far-off states and countries. Two decades and then some of stable occupation require careful archaeological work, and Caviness-Gober was focused today on what appeared to her to be an area that must have been used for non-functional creative purposes.

"I never saw so much artsy-fartsy stuff!" exclaimed Caviness-Gober, "I was sorting and cataloguing for hours and hours, when suddenly, after carefully deconstruction and removal of a clearly hand-constructed table-*esque* 'thing', for lack of a better word, BOOM! There, with pristine-ish original white surfacing, was a Lost Wall! I couldn't believe it! It was like dream, there it was rising from the surface up up up – well, not that far up because it turns out it is really just a half-wall. But still, imagine – today, there it is – a Lost Wall!"

Caviness-Gober's excitement at her own rediscovery of a Lost Wall was palpable.

"I wonder," she mused aloud to this reporter with enthusiasm, "who *were* these inhabitants, what were they like, and WHY in God's name do they have so much STUFF?? Honestly, I'm thinking about categorizing this location as a midden, because there is just no clear reason for these people to have preserved all this stuff – most of it has no discernible use in the historical record. What were they thinking when they took such pains to preserve these items, taking up so much valuable space? Did they believe these items to be supernatural? These are the questions I am determined to answer!"

After an hour or so more of sharing with this reporter similar musings, questions, and unrequited sighs of delight at her own findings, Caviness-Gober then abruptly paused.

"Oh jeez," she said sheepishly, "This happens all the time; I totally forgot something rather significant: I am 'those people' – this is all *my* stuff . . . . Well, *c'est la vie*, right? Pobody's Nerfect, if ya know what I mean. One *minor* historical fact doesn't completely invalidate an entire excavation, and/or its mellifluous findings, and/or an outstanding theory. *Right?*"

This reporter is forced to concur, because, despite the fact of the forgotten fact – which was, to be sure, a fairly significant element of the excavation project – it turned out that Caviness-Gober's long-time theory about a Lost Wall was actually correct. It *was* there all along, preserved behind the detritus, arts supplies, treasures, and crapola piled on, around, and under a long table (that she herself had constructed many years ago), upstairs in the loft of her own abode.

(*Note:* Caviness-Gober's husband could not be reached for comment on the scientific veracity of his wife's theory.)

Cabin in the Woods
Jerry Dreesen
First Place, Images Category

Driving Lesson
Radka Caviness

It is 1954. I am fifteen and eager to learn to drive. My father will teach me and I have promised my mother that no matter how impatient my father becomes, I will endure it and learn to drive.

My father has bought me a 1949 Chevrolet and had it painted black. I am thrilled. He tells me I must learn to shift *BEFORE* I ever turn the car on. That's how he learned to drive when he was in the compulsory Macedonian Army. I practice for weeks, releasing the clutch slowly, smoothly, and going through the gears. At last, with my father beside me, I drive around our neighborhood. We drive on Sundays.

After several weeks, he says I am ready to drive to Swan Island, where he works; it is a mile from our house. During the Second World War, thousands of people worked three shifts in the Oregon Shipyards at Swan Island, but now, I can practice driving in the huge nearly-empty parking lots.

We drive the half block to Going Street; a four-lane straight shot west to Swan Island. I am driving smoothly. My father is relaxed.

Strangely, there is a pile of large Douglas Fir logs across the road ahead of us.

My father says, "Do you see the logs?"

I say, "Yes."

He nods and looks out his side window.

I approach the logs and hit the gas *HARD*. The car sails through the air, clears the logs and lands with a thundering sound. I think, *great, I cleared them.*

Then, I see my father's face. His eyes are wide open. His mouth is open. He is struggling to speak. There is a moment of silence and then he begins screaming at me. Finally, he gets out of the car and looks under it. He tells me to move over, gets into the driver's side and is surprised the car starts. We drive home in explosive silence.

We are home; my father begins yelling wildly at me and tells my mother what I did.

My mother says, "Well, nothing bad happened. Anybody can make a little mistake."

My father goes ballistic. He says my mother is crazier than I am. At that moment George Nickoloff drops by. He is my father's best friend and visits often. George asks my father what is going on and my father tells him.

George turns to me and says, "Radka, did you do that?"

I say, "Yes."

George looks at me with wonder and says, "*By God,* Dushan, this is *SOME* girl. *By God,* I never heard anything so wonderful."

After he leaves, my father says George must be nuts, and he turns to me and says, "You are never driving again. I am selling your car. That's it!"

George has a tavern and unknown to us, he tells my driving story to his patrons, some of whom are Macedonian friends.

Two weeks later, the monthly Saturday evening business meeting is held at our Macedonian Club, *Podkrepa.* We arrive as usual, but as we enter, all eyes turn to us.

A group of the men, led by Sam Duman, come over and they address me (unheard of.) Duman says that they heard I jumped a logging pile with my car. Was it true? I nod yes and they immediately turn to my father and ask him to tell the wondrous story. The women nearby smile at me with pride.

After the business meeting, as we all sit at the long tables having bread, feta cheese, olives, wine, beer and soft drinks, different groups ask my father to tell the story again and again.

They all say it was a wonderful deed; that I am special. The story delights them. They say that since the car wasn't damaged, it is a sign I am favored by the Gods and because my father was a part of it, he is favored by the Gods.

I still can see their smiles and their awe. The remembering always lifts me up and makes me happy.

The next day is Sunday.

My father says, "Let's go drive."

True Haikus
Cynthia Baker

A Day
(November 14, 2017)

Neon pink sunrise
Borrowed, flowered, umbrella
Lost dog. Found! Sweet home.

A Night
(November 8, 2016)

They said, "no pathway"
Red fills the screen, state by state
We the people, vote.

My First SUP Race
(August 27, 2017)

Whistle blow! Run! Stand!
Paddle, paddle, paddle, glide.
Exhilaration.

The Fake News True Fact Seagull, its Shadow, and its Reflection

Cynthia Baker

Touché
Beth Forst

It often occurs that one is placed in the midst of rich events that one only comes to understand or relish fully years later.

Freda, my mother, was a typical 1950s mom of four; with Dad working the factory, she raised us amongst the cornfields and farms and the new housing subdivisions on the edge of suburbia of Indianapolis eastside.

I had left home to go to Indiana University. My youngest brother was in his last year in high school and the last one to eventually leave home. Kenny would play practical jokes on my mom. These stories have percolated down to morph into mom myth. Like tea bags and hot water, the stories steep.

She was a mother for 25 years; she enjoyed that last offspring's offerings of jokes and teasings, and sometimes tried to prank him back. I often received calls from mom, in which she would ask me odd questions, or I'd alleviate some worry she expressed, or she'd tell me about the latest prank exchange between her and Kenny.

"Have you seen the attachment to my vacuum cleaner?"

Odd question. Mom's closets were well-organized and I figured she had misplaced the small end piece. A week or so later she called and laughed about how Kenny had hidden it. She giggled how some turnabout with him would be funny.

Kenny had grown an interest in auto racing and kept up with local races in Indianapolis. He asked my mother if he could invite an out-of-town girlfriend to spend the weekend at the house for a particular car race. Mom agreed, and called me with questions.

"She can sleep in your bedroom. Should I tell Ken to tell Shari the plans? Do I need to have 'THE TALK' with him?"

I paused, "Seems a little late for that, don't you think?" I said with a slow chuckle.

"I may play a trick on him," she said, "I may put some *condos* under his pillow."

Sometimes silence is the best response to this sort of thing. Let it play out. Not knowing how serious she was about this potential prank, I figured she wasn't really going to follow through with it.

I called after the race weekend to see how the event went.

"Everyone had a great time. I saw it could have been embarrassing if Shari found out about the *condos* under the pillow."

"Mom, did you DO that?"

"Well, almost, but I decided to take them back."

"You took them back? Where?"

"To the drugstore. I took them to the cashier and she sent me back to talk to the Pharmacist for my cash back. He had to fill out a form with my address and then asked me the reason I was returning the item. I told him they were *too small*."

Spooky Town
Jean Roberts
(song lyric)
Honorable Mention, Song Lyric/Poetry Category

In the cool green water under the covered bridge, the mermaid is talking
to the troll
What's got under your skin, she asks? – I think I'll take a stroll
Talk to the mayor about this spot, what's okay and what is not
Spooky city! Spooky town!
The ghosts don't make a sound
Till they go OOOOOOO! EEEEEEEE! AAAAHH!

The goblin takes the trail downtown, he leaves a trail of slime
Past the homes and past the boats he walks on down the line
Finds the square, hears the echoes there, smells the smell and says –
Spooky city! Spooky town!
The ghosts don't make a sound
Till they go OOOOOOO! EEEEEEEE! AAAAHH!

There's a creak and a squeak of a window high above the square
A ghost in the tower above the old court house there
She hears the troll, she hears him wail, and she calls out to the city jail
Spooky city! Spooky town!
The ghosts don't make a sound
Till they go OOOOOOO! EEEEEEEE! AAAAHH!

A song arises from the graveyards, and all those buried trees
Lean toward city center, all those memories
Yesterday's horses and yesterday's men, all call out to us again
Spooky city! Spooky town!
The ghosts don't make a sound
Till they go OOOOOOO! EEEEEEEE! AAAAHH!

Tenacity
Cynthia Baker
Honorable Mention, Images Category

Treehouse
Alys Caviness-Gober

It is a Saturday evening in the early Fall of 1976. I'm in my freshman year in High School in Noblesville, IN.

Mike and I stand two feet apart in the treehouse that my dad and I built the summer before. My dad designed it, an A-frame ("A for Alys," he says). It stands on four sturdy 4x4 timbers cemented into the earth, with the A-frame house rising up into the embracing limbs of a huge hackberry tree. The floor of the treehouse is made of 2x4s spaced 4 inches apart for good drainage. The top third on both sides of the A-frame's peaked roof and the lower third on both sides and the front has 1x4 wood slats spaced 4 inches apart so there's always a feeling of openness, and we can always see the sunlight through the leaves and the night sky. The middle third on both sides is open – my dad says, "Picture windows, Aly," as we build it. (*Aly* is my nickname.)

Our treehouse (c. 1976)

Our first ladder up into the treehouse is simply 2x4s nailed into the tall tree trunk. Stepping the few inches from the tree into the treehouse is, for me, a split-second of terror. My mom shared my fears, worrying that my little brothers (six and eight years younger than me) will fall, so Dad adds a handmade wooden ladder at the back of the treehouse.

The front of the A-frame faces away from our house; it overlooks the last strip of our backyard and the ditch that goes down to the Nickel Plate Heritage Railway train tracks that run behind our property. The front of the treehouse has a crawl-through doorway, and the floor extends out for a slat-platform "porch" that we sit on with our legs swinging over the edge. The back of the A-frame by the tree trunk is open, and overlooks our forested yard and the back of our house. I love our treehouse.

My two younger brothers and I have sleepouts there. We build a little fire on the ground between the treehouse and the ditch that lines the railroad tracks, near where our Scarecrow stands.

Dad, Phil, & Jim working on our Scarecrow as the train rumbles by (c. 1975)

As night falls during our sleepouts, we build a fire, roast marshmallows, tell ghost stories, and when the freight trains thunder and rumble by every couple hours, we wave to the train engineers. They wave back. We love the train. When a train goes by, we wave to the whole train – we wave at the engineers, we wave at the freight cars, we wave at the caboose. Our little fire burns all night, snapping and crackling below us. After a few hours of sleep, we awake at first light and stir up its red-hot embers, in which our mom bakes fresh homemade bread in her dutch oven. The bread takes a while to cook – it seems like hours and hours – but it is worth it: we chow down the finger-burning-hot thick moist slices like starving animals.

I tell Mike about our sleepouts.

He laughs and says, "Can *I* sleep out with you?"

I know he's kidding, but I can hardly answer, I'm so nervous.

I sort of laugh and choke and stammer, "I don't think my parents would let you."

Then, I'm embarrassed: I've made it sound like *I* would let him! My head swims. Mike keeps talking; I keep pretending to listen.

The night air starts to come in, wafting through the "picture windows" and slats-sides of the treehouse, cooling my fevered brow. In the dusky light, as goosebumps shiver up and down my sweatered arms, Mike's curly blonde hair and his smile flash at me – his braces catch the fresh starlight. I can't hear his words through the roaring in my head – he is so handsome, I can scarcely breathe. He looks like a young James Cagney (who I adore). A far-off train whistle forlornly blows, adding to my excitement; I know the train will rumble by soon on the tracks behind us. I love the train so much. Again, Mike's smile flashes and makes me almost double-over – I can feel his grin stab into me. I'm terrified because I don't know how to act, but I do know: he's about to kiss me . . . and I've never been kissed before.

In a heartbeat, our sneakered toes knock into each other – I'm not sure: did he move forward or did I? I can feel his hand slide behind my back and I'm pulled into his chest. Time stands still. I feel the rough softness of his flannel shirt as I bump my cheek against him; I smell his breath sweetly swish past my nose; I see a flash of the whites of his blue eyes as mine close. I tremble. I raise my parted lips to his. The earth trembles as we kiss. Lips lightly pressing, then tongues flick and push. His tongue feels like his flannel shirt. I'm shaking, trembling, thinking, *am I doing this right?* The earth moves mightily; through my closed eyelids light flashes. Suddenly the train whistle screams as it roars down the tracks behind us! Mike and I jump ten feet in the air – we come down to earth again together, laughing. We sit in the treehouse, holding each other tightly, talking quietly. He tells me his dream for the future: he will go to Notre Dame and play football. I listen; I don't tell him I have no dreams for the future. Our occasional kisses ward off the night air for an hour or so, until my mom's voice calls us in.

That night with Mike in the treehouse was one of the few times anyone I knew came over to our house. I hadn't made many friends since my family moved from Columbus, Georgia a couple years before when I was in the middle of 7th grade. Even if I had made a lot of friends, they wouldn't have come over anyway because, well, my family just wasn't normal.

We were all long-distance runners, even my little brothers. As a family, we traveled all over the Midwest every weekend, running road races. We were also vegetarian health-nuts; our bible was Adele Davis' latest book. We didn't go Clancy's on weeknights for dinner and we didn't go to Jim Dandy's on Sundays, like everybody I knew at school did. Even worse, my family wasn't social: my parents did not join churches or clubs or get to know other parents or even our neighbors. They had each other, and they had us kids, and that was all they wanted. My brothers and I each had a few friends in the neighborhood who we rode bikes with and hung out with at the neighborhood pool, and we each had friends at school, but none of those kids came over to our house the way other kids went to each others' houses. We knew our parents' unspoken rule: "other people" weren't welcome or necessary.

For most of my life, the things that made us different were kind of okay with me; young kids don't really question their family norms. Plus, I was a shy kid; I had missed a lot of school because of my life-long lung disease. Most of my childhood was spent in doctors' offices, hospitals, or lying in my bed hour after hour hallucinating from fevers. My disease wasn't even properly diagnosed until I was almost ten years old, and with the diagnosis came the prognosis: I had three to five years to live. My prognosis, from every doctor for the rest of most of my life, was always the same. I had repeated bouts of pneumonia (up to one or two per month) for the rest of my life; doctors always said I'd be lucky to live another three to five years. They said I'd never go to college; they said I'd never get married; they said I'd never have kids. Hence my inability to share my dreams of the future with Mike that night in the treehouse: I had no dreams of the future.

Two or three years before I got diagnosed, when we still lived in the heat and humidity of Georgia, my dad started me running. He did it because he knew I was dying (from the then-undiagnosed lung problem), and he had heard Dr. Kenneth Cooper speak at Fort Benning, where my dad worked as a research psychologist. Dr. Cooper spoke about cardio-pulmonary exercise and lung health. His lecture made my dad believe running would be my salvation. When a doctor finally did diagnose my rare and incurable lung disease, we learned there was nothing "curative" to do, just lifetime antibiotics and "being careful" (don't get stressed, don't get chilled, don't get overheated, don't get exposed to common illnesses, don't don't don't – the list for controlling "my" environment was endless). My dad refused to believe what the doctors said; he believed in his own determination and he believed in Dr. Kenneth Cooper: we kept running.

Within a few years, the whole family was running, even my younger brothers Jim and Phil were running by ages five and three, respectively. Running helped my cardio-pulmonary system function and I survived, against all odds, but it changed our family. We became even odder; the anti-social vegetarian health-nut long-distance running family.

As for me, I hated every step, every breath . . . for lots of miles, for lots of years. From age eight until I stopped running as a sophomore in college, I ran a minimum of three to five miles a day. In Georgia, my dad ran with me after he got home from work. In Indiana, my mom policed me: every morning she would wake me up at the crack of dawn and say, "Time to go do your run, Alys." On school days, she'd add, "You have to hurry before the bus comes." In high school, I ran girls' track and I ran cross-country with the boys' team; there was no girls' cross-country team back then.

I was not a good runner. There is no way to accurately describe the pain involved in running with my lung disease. My lungs don't expand easily because they've been full of inflexible scar tissue and pockets of calcifications since I was four years old. The only thing that changes is how much scar tissue, how much calcification (there's always more of both after each bout of pneumonia). When I run, my lungs don't open up; they just feel like knives are slicing through them. I never "broke through the wall" or got a "runner's high." I did pass out once while running, but thankfully it was just on the track at my high school.

Me, in a late-Winter or early-Spring road race; my face says it all. (circa 1977)

No, I never enjoyed running; I never missed it after I stopped in my sophomore year of college. I remember the day I quit running like it was yesterday.

I woke up in my dorm room at Indiana University in Bloomington at my usual crack-of-dawn time, to go "do my run" before class. As always, the dorm was quiet that early in the morning. As I started to swing my legs out of bed, I thought, *Why? Why am I doing this? Mom's not here. No one will know if I just . . . stop.* So, I stopped. I didn't tell my folks for a long time, and I still ran some road races with my family on weekends. Honestly, no one could tell I had stopped training; my misery and lack of sportsy talent didn't change one bit.

Looking back, I think about all those miles, all those years I spent running. It was my own personal Hell, but . . . I have to admit, my dad and Dr. Cooper were right: running saved my life. Like I said, it also irrevocably changed my family.

With the exception of physically having to run, my family's oddness and isolation suited me when I was younger. I preferred my books and old movies to spending time with other kids. By high school, however, I longed for more friends, I wanted to be normal, I wanted to fit in – and, I wanted a boyfriend. Everybody I knew at school had a boyfriend. Mike represented so much to me. He was cool and handsome, a football star, a popular kid: he was my chance to be normal. The fact that he actually liked me was unbelievable and put me over the moon. He was my first real boyfriend, and that kiss, in my treehouse, was my first-ever kiss.

To this day, I don't remember how I talked my folks into letting Mike come over that night, let alone letting us go up into the treehouse alone. It was a one-time thing, because they never let him come over again. That was hard to explain to Mike – he took it personally – and our romance ended almost before it began. Still, for the next three and half years, when we'd pass each other in the hallways at school, we'd awkwardly smile and say hi, and always I knew: both of us still thought about that kiss.

Despite ours being a failed romance, my relationship with Mike gave me something profound, something valuable beyond a first kiss. Mike did make me feel normal for the first time in my life. Being known as his girlfriend (however briefly!) made me feel like I fit in, and I felt – finally – like I thought everybody I knew at school felt: part of a group, one of "them." That feeling was great – for about three days. Then I realized that I still felt pretty darn separate; I still liked my books and old movies more than most of my newfound friends. Being "normal" and "fitting in" and being a star football player's girlfriend (however briefly!) did not change who I was. I was still the girl whose family ran road races instead of going to church. I was still the girl who didn't have friends over. I was still the girl whose family ate vegetarian health-nut food instead of Clancy's and Jim Dandy's. And, I was still the girl who missed a lot of school because she was always sick.

By the time Mike broke up with me, it was clear to me that I was still not quite like everybody else I knew at school. Yep, my little romance with Mike gave me something even more profound than that brief period of feeling "normal." It let me realize that I was okay with being different. Actually, I was more than okay; I was happy with who I was. I was happy walking alone in the hallways at school, with an arm full of books. I was happy alone up in my treehouse, waving to the train engineers and the freight cars and the cabooses as the trains rumbled on by.

Bluegrass Heaven

Steve VandeWater
(song lyric)

I love that mountain music though I lack the skill to play
But that's all bound to change I know, come the Judgment Day.
I've always been a lousy picker, on this blessed Earth,
But up in Heaven I will play for all my soul is worth.

'Cause Heaven is the place they say, where all your dreams come true
I bet the streets are paved with gravel, and the grass is blue.
With Bill Monroe a-playin', 'cause I know he must be there
His toes a-tappin' loudly like he hasn't got a care.

So when I get to Heaven, if St. Peter lets me in
He can keep the golden harp, I'll take a mandolin
And when I get my halo and my silky wings unfurl,
I'll go and join the angel band and pick with Doc and Merle.

For Heaven is the place they say, you always get your wish.
Where creeks all flow with moonshine and there's schools o' hungry fish.
Where no one's ever hungry, nor never has to toil
A-diggin' in the cold dark mines, or workin' rocky soil.

I hope to hear good music when I've finally up and died
And Heaven is the place they say, you're always satisfied.
But what about the other folks who don't like Bluegrass well?
They sure won't be in Paradise. They'll think that they're in Hell!

But Heaven is a land where everyone gets what they want
If mine don't jive with yours perhaps I'll find a diff'rent haunt
My place is anywhere that Old Time fiddle music rings
No matter if it's hot or cold, I want to hear them strings.

So if I prove unworthy, and I end up down below,
I'll sit there by ol' Splitfoot as he rosins up his bow
We'll play there in the brimstone, flames a-dancin' all around
In the heat of Satan's campfire, barely six feet underground.

Papa Plays
Annie Oberman

Box Like Room

Maren Thornbury

Shredded paper and candy wrappers litter the floor and
the carpet is moldy and a
Starbucks cup is knocked over in the corner
spilling spoiled milk coffee all over his tattered boots.
But he just stands there and takes it,
says it adds to his 'aesthetic'.
And no one questions this but instead
with a nod and a grunt their heads fall back into their laps... and back to
the mind numbing nothingness we go.

You could float on the thickness of the silence,
until a Voice breaks out among the blind faces and
a spurt of color escapes the mouths of jaws unhinged from the disruption.
But he is just asking where the boots are from and the excitement
will die again in disappointment as there is no need to snuff out the
individuality
this time.
Yet color still touched their lips,
and in their brainless minds that is what was wrong with everything,
that is something they can't have.
So they tie him down and he understands
and doesn't protest when they rip out his tongue and
now the only color that spills out of his mouth is red.
Then when it is calm again the bodies breathe the stale air
together in perfect harmony,
hearts beat in unison,
eyes blink in sync with the sunspots.

What am I watching?

I wonder from the back of the group,
witnessing a glass bowl only one crack away from shattering all over the
kitchen floor.
It is so fragile and the system is so weak and
bland and I am so bored that
I want to scream but I cannot speak out.
For fear of the color that comes with a Voice.
They took his tongue,

and as I gingerly flick my own against the back of my teeth
I wonder if he could taste the blood after it was gone,
wonder if I could taste the soil before I die in this
prison of a box of a room.

What would it taste like?

Like freedom and life maybe,
or the sweet memory of small girl days
where we stayed outside from dawn till dusk and
swam in pink and purple ponds reflecting the fire in the sky.
It feels as if that life is fading or draining from the recollection
faster than I can fill the missing spaces and
I continue to stare into nothingness until a boy taps on the glass.

He says hello, my name is Fear,

and I am scared of what comes from the outside and sticks to your shoes,
so I lock you up in your minds and don't let you leave.
I kill your color before it spills over the side.
Because
It's just too hard to get the stains out.

And then a girl arrives,
She stands next to me with a hand on my shoulder.
I hear Her mind straining against His ideas
and she thinks nothing should contain our colors and
that nothing can.
Thinks a mess is a beautiful concept and mistakes should be made.
Thinks failure is the only option sometimes.
Her name is Courage,
She speaks to the boy with a burst of light in Her Voice.
And His eyes grow wide at the waterfall that escapes Her lips
and crashes over the small prison like box like room.
And so, He says,
you have broken everything I have built and there is nothing left inside.
And so, She said,
I will give you my heart cut up into tiny little pieces and you can use them
to mend your mind.
We are a true and colorful species.
Do not fear,
for our hearts are meant to be broken.

Florida
Casey Kenley

"You're really good at giving your kids freedom," my little sister said.

She sat beside me on a folding chair on the beach, pregnant with twins and a toddler at her feet. That's actually what she said just before it happened.

That summer in Florida, I watched my boys, 7 and 10, swim in a gray ocean after a long night of heavy storms. Ray and Leo smacked their backs into the giant waves, diving through them, letting them drag their whole bodies under the water and then erupting to the surface. The undertow pulled them fast and hard horizontally down the white beach.

Every few minutes, Ray would wave to Leo to come out of the water so they could get back in front of me where I stood so I could keep a close watch. A handful of times, I would wave them in when I felt they were getting a little too bold. Taking a book to the beach is futile when you have two little boys to watch.

I glanced up. They were too far out again. Leo was too far out. I started walking and then running toward them, waving my arms.

"Come in! Come in!" I screamed, moving into the water.

Ray began swimming toward the beach, but Leo didn't move. He was just a tiny head bobbing on top of the water. He couldn't go anywhere. I threw off my hat and sunglasses and swam as fast as I could toward him. Ray saw my panic and went back to Leo, lifting up his little brother as best he could. When I made it to Leo, I told Ray to swim directly to the beach. The waves kept coming as I held Leo. I couldn't touch the bottom of the ocean, and two giant waves took us underwater. I swam hard, telling Leo he was OK and Ray to keep swimming. When we reached the beach, we sat side by side for a long time and watched the ocean that had so quickly turned dangerous. I told them they were very brave and strong.

What Ray and Leo now refer to as "that time we almost drowned" was the most terrifying day of my life. Had I been reckless? Did I think my kids were inherently smart enough to stay out of danger? Should I have told them more about rip currents and the threat of drowning? Yes, I should have been more careful. After lunch that afternoon, I retreated to my room and had a long cry out of earshot of my kids.

Rearview Mirror

Gail Mehlan

October 10, 2017

Walking with this heavy baggage is getting more and more difficult for me. Panic sets in. My heart beats quickly, feeling like it will jump out of my body. It is piercingly cold outside, I am wearing a warm coat that is weighing heavy on my shoulders, adding to my burden. Underneath my coat, I am soaked in sweat. I have a strong feeling that I will be late if I don't hurry, so I press on, looking for the station, looking for the way…fearful that I will miss it and be left here. I think to myself, I can make it if I drop a bag or two, but I don't know what to leave behind. I keep going, dragging these bags, moving forward.

The station is busy this afternoon and people are all around me, pushing and disgruntled. Everyone seems to have someplace to go. It appears to me that everyone's place is more important than where I am going. I disagree.

"Hurry up!"

"Step this way! Get in this line. Buy a ticket!"

"Get out of the way!"

Today is a very important day. Something big is going to happen today. No one can possibly know or understand the real truth of the matter. I need to get somewhere else. It is imperative that I make it. This sense of urgency leaves me with a pit in my stomach.

I sling my purse and another heavy duffle bag over my shoulders and pull a suitcase with each hand. My suitcases both feel like they are full of rocks or books. Even though they have roller wheels, they feel like they do not move. Ugh! I look behind me and see that I have one more bag to grab. I try to slip it somehow over the other suitcase handle so that I can proceed in line, but it keeps falling off and making the suitcase uneven so it is constantly tipping. Feeling frustrated, I finally inch forward slowly. Someone rudely bumps my arm and my heavy purse drops off of my shoulder. Struggling, I get it back up on my shoulder. I am alone. This is all my responsibility, the carrying of these enormous bags.

As soon as I approach the front of the line, I glance up at the sign. I don't understand exactly what it says, but realize with discouragement, that this is not the station. I cannot get to where I need to go from here. I begin to slowly work my way around the crowd and down to the next block, laboriously dragging my heavy luggage with me. Feeling the pressure of people pushing in on me. I feel desperate. These bags seem so very heavy!

Then in the corner of my eye, I see a cab going by. I decide to step out to the curb, dragging the bags, and hail a cab. Perhaps I will make it if I get a cab, I think.

One by one cabs fly by me, "occupied" or "not for hire." I stand on the corner feeling more and more frustrated. I have that hopeless sense that this situation is so bad that I can't possibly make it. Suddenly a cab finally stops. It takes all of my strength to lift the burden of my bags into the trunk and a few into the cab itself. We take off…perhaps I will make it after all. My heart feels a glimmer of possibility.

Riding in the cab is not the answer to my problem. We seem to be going too fast. The cabbie seems to have lost his way. Suddenly it is pitch black outside and rain and sleet are pelting down on the windshield. There is no way the driver can see ahead of us. I try to look forward to see if I can see. Black. It is nothing but darkness, completely black. A sense of sadness overcomes me. My eyes brim over with tears and my head starts to pound.

Then I notice the rearview mirror. I find myself straining up over the front seat to see the mirror. As I'm looking in the rearview mirror and I see myself….

In the mirror, I can see *behind* me. I see the road behind me and myself clearly. I see images of the life I have lived. Images flash in the mirror before me, images of things that have happened. Nothing that's ahead. I keep struggling to look up at the mirror. Wanting to see more, wanting to go back.

Suddenly the frantic attempts to find the station dissolve. I look up and discover that I'm already at the station. I don't have to go anywhere else to get where I need to go. I am where I need to be. I will make it home. I sigh with relief as tears of gratitude slowly roll down my cheeks.

Then I wake up.

The dream leaves me with a horrible headache and "still-in-my-brain" fogginess along with a sense of immense sadness. When I am finally fully up, the dream still on my mind, I begin to think. Sometimes I think too much. But I want to understand. This dream has a meaning. Someone, something is speaking to me.

I ask myself some serious questions.

What does this mean?
What am I afraid of?
Why the overwhelming feeling of sadness?
What is all this baggage I'm trying to carry?
Am I fearful and sad for an unknown future?
Why all the searching, working, reaching, striving to get somewhere different?
Why the struggle when so much is right here, in this moment, this place, this time?
Is it normal to feel this inexplicable sadness?
Is it a letting-go of my perfect "image" of life?
Am I grieving my expectations? My unfulfilled expectations?

I work at it, trying to get to some answers and shake the foggy feelings. I finally convince myself to just go about my day, breathing, letting God be in charge. I ask Him to take the heavy baggage, whatever it may be, and to show me that the station is right where I am…to take me home.

There is no need to live life looking in the rearview mirror.

Lost and Found

Arlene Barker

I thought I got lost a lot when streets were mostly straight, before some evil magician began to bend them into circles and squiggles and serpent-like twists, making navigation even more confusing for a four-directional traveler like me. I now hesitate to venture out to anywhere new or unknown, afraid I will be swallowed up into some twirly asphalt vortex. I guess I'm just a linear person in a twisteroo world.

But is life just getting from starting point to finish, is it? If that was the case, I guess it would be good to be the proverbial crow who supposedly flies as an arrow in the straightest shortest line from one point to another. Of course, crow moves are unencumbered by gravity's glue. Bypassing earthly roads, barricades, and detours with air and sky options, he can set his sights and fly directly to his destination. That ability sure would come in handy during my frequent travels with my daughter, Kelli.

Kelli's moves have taken us from Indy to Arizona, North Carolina, DC, Colorado, and some in-betweens. Snug in her little white Civic with the duct-taped bumper, we've maneuvered our way through highways, byways, and life, sometimes referring to ourselves as *Thelma* and *Louise*, although the film's unfortunate ending does make that a dubious comparison.

On our trips, I typically play the role of the crow who just sees the destination. Kelli, on the other hand, has never met a historical marker, home-town "museum," or scenic overlook she can resist, even if it means going out of her way, and sometimes getting a little bit lost. So when she moves from Arizona, the family meets up in Colorado, and I happily agree to be her co-pilot on the drive back to Indy. Not being the "as the crow flies" type of gal, she announces her intention to go home by way of Mt. Rushmore! Huh?

"Oh...kay. Maybe that will be interesting. I guess that's something I've always wanted to see?" I reply.

I imagine how much longer the drive will take, not to mention how many more miles the '93 Civic has left in it. We begin the drive with maps and Kelli, the human compass, navigating – as usual.

Making our way up the long winding roads of the Black Hills to reach Mt. Rushmore proves to be a nail-biter. We discover that thick fog and twisting mountain roads are not happy companions, with no place for U-turns. I look to those big rocky faces to give us encouragement, but the closer we get reality sets in. The four stony-faced leaders have disappeared, hiding under a cloudy gray blanket with just one nostril of Washington's nose peeking out!

When we finally reach the museum at the top of the mountain we can't see a thing, but we find it all pretty laughable, and maybe even more memorable than if our original goal had been achieved. After a picture or two in front of the foggy mountainside, we begin twisting our way down, leaving the rest of Washington's ample nose and his buddies for another visit.

We find the Badlands asleep under a blanket as well. Through the fog, they appear just barely naughty, so we start the long drive through a whole lot of empty space in South Dakota. Just when we wonder if we are the only two people in the world...

"Is that a police car?" Kelli asks.

It seems to appear out of nowhere.

"Yes!" I reply, "Where did he come from? Were you speeding?"

Suddenly *Thelma and Louise* pops into my head.

A sturdy but pleasant looking officer with a silver star and an oversized round-brimmed hat has to bend down considerably to peek into the open Civic window. He looks curiously at my curly-haired daughter and me, the older anxious-looking woman beside her.

"Are you ladies lost?" he asks.

I'm sure he notices the out-of state plates.

Now, there's no such thing as being lost in Kelli-world. She's always just "exploring more interesting routes," but she plays along and replies, "Maybe just a little."

The trooper takes pity on us, and kindly gives directions that Kelli may or may not follow. We continue on our way, making a few more errant turns here and there, but eventually arriving back to Indy in one piece with several Mt. Rushmore postcards.

Although the Civic has been replaced, and the destinations have varied through the years, it is always the same – the two of us listening to decades of our favorite music while discovering scenes of quiet beauty, quirky tourist road-stands, and each other – especially each other – because you can never really feel lost when someone you love is in the seat beside you.

I'm still not good at directions, but I've learned life is not just getting from start to finish. Flying like that old straight-as-an-arrow crow might be quicker, but birds also dip their wings and arc and glide slowly over beautiful landscapes – vistas perhaps unseen on those swift straight journeys when eyes and heart are focused only on ending destinations.

My wise daughter has taught me that maybe it's okay to not always know exactly where you're going – to get twisted around and even lost. Sometimes, when you think you've lost your way, you've really just dipped your wings and found a glorious new place where you never even realized you wanted to go.

Candy Crush
Sarah E. Morin

When Mindy was in the 5th grade, she fell irrevocably in love with Scott Adams. It didn't matter that she'd hit her growth spurt and now towered nine inches over him. It didn't matter the only thing they had in common was car rides that always ran late, giving them twenty precious minutes every day after school to shoot hoops. They weren't even in the same classroom. It even didn't matter that he had no inkling of her undying devotion.

Well, it sort of mattered, but she lacked the words to tell him.

Until she saw the conversation hearts.

They appeared in the drug store holiday aisle in early January. There, beside the wilting after-Christmas bargains, rose a new monument to holiday commercialization: the Valentine's Day display. Roses, cards, stuffed monkeys smooching each other with magnetic lips. Mindy's head played the music from *2001: A Space Odyssey.* This was her obelisk, appearing to invite her into a new phase of being. Into the world of grown-ups and shiny Russell Stover boxes.

But a box of four chocolates in the Tiniest, Cutest Box Ever still cost $4.99. She didn't love Scott Adams *that* much. And she still had to buy Garfield and Friends valentines for the rest of the class. You had to buy them for everyone, but she knew how to play the game. You saved the pretty purple Garfield ones for your best friends. The boys who annoyed you got Odie.

Scott Adams deserved more than Odie. But how to tell him the words written on her adolescent heart?

She'd give him a box of conversation hearts.

They were perfect. A pink box of hard candies. They looked like pastel chalk compressed into heart shapes. On each was written an eloquent message proclaiming such profound sentiments as:

COOL
HI BABY

XOXO

Oh, they were the 5th grade version of a Shakespearean sonnet, written in colored sugar.

Mindy saved her allowance for two weeks. It took her until February 13th to muster her courage to actually make the purchase. She did it by pretending to need to use the bathroom while her mom was shopping in the grocery store next door. She stood very straight and tall in the checkout line and released the warm, sweaty coins from her grip onto the counter. The matronly clerk smiled a doting smile. Mindy adjusted her scrungie to look more mature.

"You're short five cents, hon," said the sales clerk. "Sales tax."

Oh this strange adult world, full of valentines and taxes! Mindy dug in her pockets and came up with lint and a mini basketball.

"Miiiindy!"

Her older brother Dave and his friend Leyton strode through the door, their hair still damp from basketball practice. She smelled the boy-smell before she saw them behind her: gym socks and ranch Doritos.

"There you are. You're in trouble with Mom, you know," said her brother.

"Watcha buyin?" said Leyton. He was a spidery red-haired thing, all legs and arms and mischief.

Mindy slapped her palm down over the box of conversation hearts. "Nothing."

Leyton poked at her hand. She poked him back. The moment she lifted her hand Dave snatched the box.

"Oooooooo," Dave taunted in a sing-song voice.
The sales clerk eyed the line behind them. "Hon, do you have five cents or not?"

Mindy tried her best "angelic baby sister" look on her brother. "Give me five cents? I'll repay you ten cents at home."

"Fifty cents or I'll tell Mom you bought candy for your booooyfriend."

"A quarter and I won't tell everyone you love Gretchen Baker."

"I do not!"

Leyton rolled his eyes and slapped a nickel down on the counter. "Who's it for, anyway?"

"No one!"

Dave made smooching sounds.

Leyton eyed them both, then tugged on Dave's elbow. "Come on, let's go to your house and order that pizza, man."

Mindy jammed the box into her back jeans pocket. The box only had one dented corner when Mindy reached the safety of her room. It had not damaged the back of the box, with the giant red heart surrounding a TO and FROM. She spent the next three hours picking out the right color pen for her inscription. Definitely nothing with glitter. She picked a blue BIC pen as her Cupid's arrow and scratched her name and her beloved's in her spiral bound notebook. She practiced disguising her handwriting.

TO: The sweetest person in the 5th grade
FROM: Your Secret Admirer

Her hand trembled as she put pen to the pink box. Suddenly the door burst open.

"Ack!" she flung the pen into the air.

It flew across the room and hit Leyton on the nose.

Dave spoke up from beside Leyton. "You owe us a quarter."

She raided the intestines of her piggy bank. When she turned back, the boys were examining the box of candy.

"Give that back!" she snatched it away.

Dave sang. "Mindy and a monkey sittin' in a tree. K-I-S-S-I-N—"

The "G" was muffled by the door she slammed in their faces.

"You hit my nose again!" said Leyton.

"Good!"

She started in again on the inscription. Oh no! When the boys barged in she'd jerked a long line of ink through the heart. Eek!

Knock knock knock.

"Go away!"

"It's Leyton! I just want to return that book."

He ducked when he opened the door, as though expecting more low-flying pens.

"So where's the book?" she asked.

He put his hands in his pockets and shrugged. "Actually I wanted to borrow the next in the series."

Mindy fought a smug smile. "I *told* you it was good."

"Yeah, except the ending. The captain gets eaten by a sea monster? Really?"

"Yeah, so sad. Now Lady Amelia will have to run the pirate ship without him."

"No, I mean he so could have taken that sea monster down."

They debated the prowess of sea monsters for a couple minutes. She didn't realize she'd dropped her guard as he approached, so now he could see the back of the box.

She blushed, but well, he'd seen it already. "See what you two made me do?"

"Oh, that's easy to fix. Gimme your pen. A spear tip at one end, some feather lines at the other and ta-da!"

He'd made the pen scratch into a Cupid's bow, piercing the heart.

"Amazing!"

Leyton puffed out his thin chest. "I know I am." He lowered the pen to the box again. "To Leyton, because you are *amaaaazing.*"

She shoved him out the door.

"You still owe me a quarter."

"You'll get it tomorrow at school."

But the next day she was far too nervous to think of quarters for Leyton. It was THE DAY. Valentine's Day. She called Lizzie before school to ask to borrow her red IU hoodie.

"But you're a Purdue fan," said Lizzie.

"We're supposed to wear red for the class party."

She slipped Lizzie's hoodie on before class. The kangaroo pouch in front was perfect – just the right size for a box of conversation hearts. They rattled when she shot hoops at recess. So she had to abandon a perfectly good game of HORSE, which she was, for once, winning against Scott and Leyton.

Mindy spent the entire class party in a cold sweat. She didn't eat her cupcake because it dyed her tongue purple. What if Scott smiled at her in the hallway and she smiled back and her teeth were bright purple? Like Leyton, who turned around in his desk and flashed her an impish violet grin.

"You gonna eat that?"

"Take it. But then I don't owe you a quarter anymore."

He considered this and swiped her cupcake.

Lizzie eyed her. "Are you feeling all right, Mindy?"

"She's looovesick," Leyton said through a mouthful of mushy, half chewed chocolate crumbs. Disgusting.

"Put your valentines in your backpacks now." Their teacher, Mr. Jones, patted his stomach. "If I catch you with candy during the rest of class, it's mine."

Oh no. Now Mindy was breaking the law.

Then the fateful hour arrived.

The 5th grade switched classrooms for math, which meant trekking across the hall to Mrs. Dickenson's classroom. Which also was Scott Adams's homeroom. Where Mindy sat in Scott Adams's desk every day for forty blissful minutes, full of the tantalizing notion that his buttcheeks had been the ones to warm the plastic seat for her.

It had to be Fate that assigned her to Scott Adams's desk. Then again, Fate must be cruel because it had also seated Leyton to her right. He kept smirking at her, so she turned her back to him and toward Krissy, the class tattletale, on her other side.

Krissy stuck her prissy hand in the air. "Miz Dickenson! Mindy's trying to cheat off my quiz!"

Mrs. Dickenson ordered Mindy to swivel back around.

Mindy scribbled a few random answers on her quiz, sidled her eyes right and left. She slid her hands into the kangaroo pouch of the IU sweatshirt. Her damp palms closed around the thin cardboard box.

The clock ticked overhead like a bomb timer.

She lifted the desk lid, millimeter by millimeter.

Creeeeeak went the hinges.

It seemed to echo like that time her family hollered into the Grand Canyon. But the only one who seemed to have noticed was Leyton.

He stared at her hand, eyes wide. What? Didn't he think she had the guts to deliver a stupid valentine? She'd show him! She shoved the box into Scott's desk.

The candy rattled on impact.

"Miz Dickenson!" Krissy waved her hand in the air again, her butt halfway off her seat. "Mindy's stealing something outta that desk."

Mindy snatched her hand back. The lid banged close.

She couldn't lift her head but she could feel the gazes on her, like headlights. Clack clack clack went Mrs. Dickenson's hard-heeled shoes on the tiles. They parked in front of Mindy, all shiny and black like cop cars.

"I didn't take anything," Mindy mumbled.

"But your hands were in another student's desk?"

Mrs. Dickenson slowly opened the lid. *Creeeeeak.*

After a long pause, Mrs. Dickenson said, "I don't see anything missing."

Mindy's head shot up. Mrs. Dickenson's eyes looked sympathetic.

Krissy's uptight curls sprang into Mindy's field of vision.

"What's that?" She grabbed the box and read it aloud to the class. "To the sweetest person in the 5th grade. From Your Secret Admirer."

Mindy was certain her face matched her red IU hoodie.

"Oh thanks, loudmouth, now you ruined my prank," said Leyton.

Krissy's pursed lips gaped open. "You put this in there?"

"Yeah, I was going to get him back for shaving my cat by giving him a fake girlfriend. Now everyone's gonna know it's not real. Thanks a lot."

Mrs. Dickenson plucked the box from Krissy's grasp. "You shouldn't have had your hands in another student's desk, either, Leyton."

"I didn't. I got Mindy to do it for me."

"Then you can both stay after class. And that will be the end of that. If you will all pass your quizzes to the front –"

The teacher clacked back to her desk. Leyton leaned over and whispered, "Soooo…Scott Adams? Really?"

But she'd had enough conversation – and conversation hearts – for now.

Seven Years Later…

Mindy opened her locker. It was so crammed full of books and notes she didn't see the tiny pink box until it toppled out onto the floor.

Lizzie stopped rambling about the latest episode of Buffy long enough to scoop it up.

"You holding out on me? Who gave you conversation hearts?" Lizzie jumped up and down. "It was Scott Adams, wasn't it?"

"How'd those get in my locker?"

"You gave Scott your locker combination last month so he could return your Basketball Blunders tape, remember?" Lizzie squealed. "Oh look, he wrote something on the back."

To the sweetest person at Shelbyville High School. From your Secret Admirer.

Lizzie went into sonic. "Eeeeeeeeee! It has to be Scott. Who else would remember?"

"You remembered," Mindy pointed out. Her heart pounded like a basketball being dribbled across the court for a desperate half court buzzer shot.

Lizzie picked at the top. "The box is taped shut. I bet there's a present inside."

But there wasn't. There were just the normal chalky candies. Only someone had scratched some of the letters off each heart.

"It's a secret message!" Lizzie plunked herself down in the middle of the hallway and spread the candies out before her.

Five minutes later, they'd spelled out DANCE WITH ME.

Lizzie tackled Mindy and sent the candies ricocheting off the lockers. "You're going to the Valentine's Day Dance Friday with Scott Adams! I can't believe it finally happened."

"We don't know it's Scott. And I'm not going to the dance."

But there was no saying no to Lizzie. Her best friend kidnapped her to go dress shopping on Tuesday. On Wednesday there was another box of conversation hearts in her locker, this time spelling out PIC U UP AT SIX.

She had to admit, even in her confusion, she was getting excited. She'd given up on Scott Adams years ago. They didn't have anything in common except basketball. She'd tried to engage him in conversation about books, politics, and art, but he was a man with one theme. Still, he was super-nice. Maybe he'd been shy around her all this time and hidden his deeper self.

That was it, she decided as she adjusted her hoop earrings. She practiced her face in the hall mirror. How should she look when she opened the door? Surprised? Delighted? Sexy?

"What are you doing?"

She jumped. "Leyton?"

Dave hadn't mentioned he was coming by. Maybe – to borrow that tux he was wearing? Leyton never went to school dances, but where else did a guy wear a tux? He looked good in it, just not – like mischievous Leyton.

"If you keep doing that your face is gonna get stuck," Leyton said.

She bonked him.

"This is why I'm so attracted to you. Your feminine reserve."

She elbowed him on her way to the coat closet. "Shut up and pass me those shoes."

"Which ones?"

She glanced over at the red heels, dyed to match her dress perfectly. "The combat boots, whaddaya think?"

"Dare you." He smirked but set the shoes before her.

She steadied herself on his arm as she slipped them on. "Hey, did you finish the book I lent you?"

"How could I? There are no pictures in it."

"Leyton, you read more than I do."

"Yes, I finished it. Loved the main character. The ending was stupid though. Why'd she have to die?"

"It was poetic!" she protested.

The debate raged until the clock struck the quarter hour. Scott was late. Maybe he'd driven by and seen Leyton's car in the drive.

She rose from the sofa. "This has been fun and all but perhaps it's time to go."

"Hot date tonight?" he arched a brow. "Nah, you're right. And I have a beautiful woman to escort to the dance. Even cleaned the car for her."

"Yeah, that means tossing the Taco Bell wrappers in the back."

He grinned and picked up her coat. For a moment she thought he was going to play keep away with it, and for sure she'd lose in heels, but he spread it open to help her into it. Weird. Not a bad weird, just, confusing. Like the brief brush of his fingers against her bare arm as she slid her left arm into the coat.

She shook herself. "So did you leave the book in your car? You probably have time to bring it in before you go."

"Before...*we* go?"

"Well, I'll see you there, but Scott's picking me up."

The coat behind her froze midair. She fished for the right arm hole.

"You're going to the dance with...Scott?"

"Oh yeah, I didn't tell you. You remember that time in the 5th grade when I tried to sneak the conversation hearts into his desk? Well, he's been passing me notes all week through – get this – boxes of conversation hearts. I keep finding them in my locker."

"Oh."

She turned to face him. "What, the idea of the best athlete in school wanting to take me to a dance sends you into shock? I am All-State, you know."

Leyton shook his head carefully, as though too abrupt a motion might rattle his brain. "No, you're right. You and Scott. You have lots in common."

Yeah, they had basketball and...basketball.

"And you've always had that crush on him."

"Hey, I never thanked you for pretending that box was your idea of a prank back in the fifth grade. Saved me a lot of embarrassment."

"Yeah, nothing's worse than embarrassment." He scratched his collar. "Um, well, I guess I'll go –"

He'd only been gone a moment when she remembered, she hadn't gotten the book back. She rushed outside.

Crunch went something under her foot. She nearly toppled off her high heels. She bent to the ground. Pastel chalk dust?

No, a crushed conversation heart.

And two feet away, another, intact. She picked it up. Then another. Hearts trailed all the way down the sidewalk and drive to… Leyton's car.

She spotted his lanky silhouette in the porchlight. He was leaning against the driver's door, looking out onto the street.

"Leyton?" she whispered.

He tensed, then slowly turned. She knew that guilty look of chagrin.

She held out her handful of hearts.

"Some prank, eh?" he mumbled.

Her heart whammed. "Prank?"

"Scott's not coming, Mindy."

"*Prank?*" She pelted him with a faceful of candy. "You mean this was you?"

He nodded.

"You set this all up to make fun of me!" She whirled around to run back inside.

"No, Mindy, wait!" he grabbed her shoulder. She pivoted to face him, but stayed out of reach.

"What was going to happen after this, Leyton? I wait around all evening for some 'Secret Admirer' who doesn't show?"

"Your Secret Admirer did show! I guess I just didn't realize how secret I was!"

"He d–" The words hit. She blinked. "What?"

"If anyone knows how to hide a crush, it's you. I thought for sure you'd figured it out."

Her voice sounded tinny. "Figured out what?"

"That I've had a crush on you since the 5ᵗʰ grade."

She couldn't squeeze enough air out of her lungs. "But you were always teasing me."

He arched his brow as if to say, *well, duh.*

The memory of Valentine's Day in the 5ᵗʰ grade, and everything since, replayed like home video in her head. Only this time, the camera angles were different. Leyton, coming over not just to visit her brother but to borrow her books. Leyton, pushing her to compete in basketball, in class. Leyton drawing the arrow to fix the ink mark on the box of candy. Leyton staring at her, wide-eyed, when he saw her reaching to drop the candy into *Scott's* desk and not –

"You thought I bought those hearts for you," she whispered.

Was he blushing? She couldn't tell in the dim porch light.

"Nevermind. It was stupid. You don't want me, you want Scott. I'm sorry I got your hopes up."

"Leyton, wait –" She took a step toward him. *Crunch.* She'd tread on the scattering of candy she'd thrown at him.

Leyton looked down at the crushed heart. "Well, there's your favorite kind of ending. Tragic and poetic."

But she only halfway heard him, because she was trying to stay upright. She'd never had much need for high heels, and wasn't used to balancing on them – or a pile of hard candies. She toppled.

Leyton dove. He was too late to catch her, but he made an excellent landing pad.

"Sorry!" she said. "You ok?"

"No, I'm dead," Leyton said melodramatically, face buried in the pavement. "You ok?"

"Uh-huh." She rolled off him and he sat up slowly. She couldn't help it. She snorted a laugh.

"What?"

"Your tux – it's covered in pastel candy dust."

"And here I wasn't going to mention the candy dust all over your backside."

She chased her own tail. "You serious?"

"Yes."

"With you I never know. Hey! Quit looking!" She covered her rear with her hands.

He obediently rolled his eyes up to the stars, but she could tell he was biting back a grin.

"I guess we can't go to the dance now," she said.

His eyes latched on to hers. "We?"

"Um…" She replayed the home video of Leyton in her mind again, 5th grade and all the years that came after. "Ok, I've had about two minutes to think about you in this new light. But if I had known it was you asking me to the dance, Leyton, I probably would have said yes."

A slow smile spread across his face. His hands sought pants pockets that weren't there. "So…what do we do now? All dressed up and nowhere – "

"Oh, I think we're up to standards for the Taco Bell Drive-Thruogh."

"Hot sauce!" he skipped to the passenger door and opened it for her. "But I'm buying."

They ran over one more candy heart as they backed out of the driveway, but neither noticed. They were already too deep in a sweet new conversation.

Sunflowers
Annie Oberman

I Don't Think We Will

Mike Stewart (song lyric)

Back before I went to war, or really, anywhere
I took my first trip to the West to see what's happening there
With my friend Dan who had himself a Plymouth muscle car
Two young fools flying low, not caring where we are
Screaming out Route 66 when that could still be done
A pair of hickish hellions, hell bent on having fun

Dan was drinking PBR and I was smoking hash
We'd sold our childhood homestead, so I had a little cash
We were heading to Las Vegas, checking all points in between
Awestruck by the scenery – stuff we'd only seen
On TV and in movies, or in a magazine
Each new place more happening than the place where we'd just been

Altered states through other states, no regard for the law
Taking over ownership of everything we saw
Racing headlong into places trouble always dwells
A danger to the general public – a danger to ourselves
Not thinking of the consequences, just two stupid kids
Should of thought about that, but I don't think we did

While driving through the desert, we came upon a storm
Bright sunshine on either side, the middle filled with harm
Thunder, lightning, sheets of rain, wind blowing us around
When lightning struck beside us, I swear we left the ground
You could feel the thunder crashing; we were pelted by the hail
Two new lost explorers in the middle of a gale

Then, all of a sudden; we were on the other side
The sun was shining bright again; the road had nearly dried
Soaked up by the desert, soaked up by my brain
The fury of that storm, where I thought it never rained
"Did that really happen Dan, or am I just too high?"
He said, "For a minute there I thought; we're going to die."

Emboldened by the spectacle we had just survived
We thought we were invincible, so we then contrived
To turn around and go back through it from the other side

Chase the rush of another turn on nature's carny ride
But this time with the top down and I'll sit on the hood
Dan said, "Yeah that sounds like fun, but I don't think we should."

In Winslow, Arizona, we met up with Sheriff Sam
Driving just a little quick; Sam saw Dan lift his can
His bubble light was flashing as he pulled us to the side
I tried to think of all the things I had I'd better hide
But I was focused on that storm; couldn't get it off my mind
So, there's just no telling what Sheriff Sam might find

Then Dan got out and in Sam's face and started raising hell
I though we're going to Vegas, now I think we're going to jail
Then Sam tapped on the window and asked me to roll it down
And asked what I thought I was doing in his Winslow town
I mumbled incoherently; words I could not form
I was looking up at Sam, but I was thinking 'bout that storm

Sam said, "Son, I think you're worse than the other guy
Go drink some coffee, sober up and I might let you by."
So, we walked into the Golden Bear and got a cup to go
Then stood out on the corner and watched the traffic flow
Waving to the pretty girls but none of them slowed down
We weren't quite as lucky as that handsome Jackson Browne

After 'bout an hour, Sheriff Sam returned
We walked the line and told him 'bout the lesson we had learned
He said, "Alright, you seem OK, now get on out of town."
We coasted to the city limit, then put the hammer down
Screeching tires, a cloud of smoke; we were on our way
Two new reckless outlaws made a fishtailed getaway

But as soon as we hit Vegas, we were detained once again
They were acting on a tip, we thought, from our Sheriff friend
They shook us down then let us go; there's nothing they could prove
So, we headed straight down to the strip to find our Vegas groove
We gambled lots of money and saw some girly shows
But after a few days of this, it was time to go

We made it back in record time – no roadside stops at all
If we had been entered, we'd have won the Cannonball
Years later I ran into Dan, back here where we belong

I said, "I think about that trip each time I hear that song."
Dan said, "Me too. We should relive the wonder and the thrill."
I said, "Sure, let's do it." But, I don't think we will.

Indiana October

Annie Oberman

Indiana October
Indiana October
Oh, how I love you so!
With your chilly breeze
And changing leaves
With yellows and reds aglow.
Indiana October
Indiana October
Oh, what cherished delight!
With your comfort food
And harvest moon
Lighting the sky at night.
Indiana October
Indiana October
Oh, how my heart does sing!
With apple pies baking
And leaf piles raking
Oh, what a beautiful thing!

Gravity's Curse

John Gilmore
(song lyric)

Walking along and what'd I see
a big old crow perched high in a tree
I stopped and looked up at that crow in the tree
he cocked his head and looked back at me

I said "Mr Crow, hey how do you do"
He said "my featherless friend, I'm fine. How 'bout you"
I said "Things are tough down here down on the ground.
With the weight of the world the troubles abound

Then the crow rose up and caught the West Wind
Would he ever be back. Would he land here again
I said "Mr Crow, how I wish I were you"
And as he flew out of sight, I bid him adieu

So here I am stuck down here on Earth
Oh, but I can dream for whatever it's worth
about risin' up and catching a breeze
and floating away to where ever I please.

Praying
Annie Oberman
Tie for *Third Place*, Images Category

The Magic House

Alys Caviness-Gober

29 June 2014

Hiya Dad,

Mom and Jim drove by our old house yesterday; it was a whim, I guess. Mom has never even driven by it, not once in twenty-six years, even though you guys lived only a quarter a mile away from it all that time. You know she never wanted to move; we all thought it was a crazy thing you did, upsizing to a bigger home, after we were all grown and moved out. Anyway, they said the old house looked kind of abandoned, so Mom and I decided to went back today, after our train ride, to see if any of the neighbors know what's going on with the house. I almost wish we hadn't gone on the train ride. Our beloved train. It was just too emotionally hard for all of us. We felt too keenly the missing person. *You*, Dad. I cried as we passed our old backyard at the old house. Remember, Dad, how much we loved it when the train went by? It just made me miss you more.

Anyway, hocus-pocus is real, Dad. I did take Mom to the old house after the train ride. It *did* look abandoned; the grass was long and unkempt, there were vines growing in the gutters. We talked to the neighbors on both sides; both new folks since we lived there. They told us the man who owned it had died two and half years ago and his son had been living there, alone, but he hadn't done well. The bank was about to foreclose, the Homeowners' Association had just filed a lien for unpaid dues. The neighbors also told us when the man had died; his stroke was in the same week you had your first stroke two and a half years ago. The man's brother is the executor of the estate; he evicted his own nephew the very week you died. It is as though that house sat there for two and a half years, waiting, waiting for you to pass away, waiting for Mom to be able to come home to it.

Mom and I looked in the front windows. Dad, her wooden inside-shutters in the living room and dining room are still there. We walked around to the back. Our beautiful forest is gone, someone cut down ALL the trees. Our wonderful A-frame treehouse that you designed and built is gone. They put in a really nice three-season screened porch, though. Nice thick wood, beautiful. Mom and I went into the porch. We peered into the kitchen; our old sliding glass double door's been replaced by wide French-door style panes of glass, one of which is a door, and suddenly my hand was reaching for the door handle. Dad, as I was reaching, I was thinking to myself, *what the **hell** are you doing* and as I grasped the door handle, Mom was saying, "Alys, what are you doing, that's not going to –" but she never finished the sentence because THE HANDLE TURNED AND THE DOOR OPENED.

Dad, we were shocked speechless, but we both knew: that was YOU making my hand reach for that handle, that was you turning my hand and opening that door. That was you, saying to Mom, *Ok, Radka, you win; it is time to come home.*

Dad, you know the rest. We walked through our old house. It's hard to describe how we felt, it was crazy familiar and strangely surreal to see all the sameness and the changes: "our" plain white walls were painted with a color scheme that was all bizarre shades of "baby poop" (seriously, every possible disgusting shade of baby poop you can imagine). Your walnut paneling in the fireplace room was covered over by regular drywall and painted a poopy salmon, and my old bedroom was painted blood red (that had to be the son's bedroom, right?!). It was crazy. But it was *still home*. All your shelving in the closets and garage were still there. Your big bathroom mirrors were still there. So much was exactly the same. I knew immediately that if there was any way to get that house for Mom, we would do it.
Love,
Alys

25 July 2014
Hiya Dad,
The old house odyssey is a journey of miracles, obstacles, and moments indescribable. Mom asked Jim to move Heaven and Earth, and you know, Dad, that Jim'll move Heaven and Earth to get the house for her. The shenanigans involved in this particular sale are unimportant now, but I will say (knowing you would agree): the realtor was an ass, the executor-brother was an ass. It was obvious that they weren't going to clean a thing, fix a thing, yet they acted like the house was worth market value. Jim and Phil did negotiations back and forth with the realtor, At one point, we were all prepared to walk away, even Mom said, "this is too much" ("this" being the realtor's and executor/brother's attitudes). But, we all knew: Mom's heart was set on the old house; she wanted to go home. On 16 July 2014, Jim called me to tell me the deal was done and the old house was hers. I'm the one who got to tell Mom; we both cried, and she kept saying over and over, "Are you telling me I get to *go home?*" and I kept saying, "Yes, Jim and Phil did it."

We were not wrong about the hocus-pocus signs, Dad. Jim and Mom driving by, my hand reaching for that door handle and opening that door, us walking through the house, finding out the timing involved in the man's stroke and death and the eviction of the son, just all of it. The hocus-pocus signs that it was meant to be. Mom and I, we believe in destiny. The next day, I took the earnest money to the realtor's office.

The house is in pretty good shape, but there's a lot to do. Jim's coming back for a week, right after John leaves for Germany. Jim, Phil, and I'll get it all done. In the meantime, Dad, you should know that your boys were perfection. They both did their best for our Mom. I know you are proud of them.
Love,
Alys

24 August 2014
Hiya Dad,
Today John left for his year at the University in Germany. The past few weeks have been a blur of preparation, last minute obstacles to overcome, and trying hard to show John only sincere happiness for his great adventure. I cry when I am alone, though. I told Aly that she can't go anywhere for a year; I can't take it if she is also too far away for me to hug. This sense of loss is overwhelming; we just lost you two months ago; now I've "lost" John for a year. I want so much to hear him bounding down the stairs. Dad, I miss him so much already.

It's still hard to go to your big house to help Mom pack up and **not** see you in the little laundry room window or to walk in and **not** find you in one of your chairs. How must Mom feel, there in that big house where you're everywhere? I can't wait to get her into the old house.
Love,
Alys

08 September 2014
Hiya Dad,
Jim and Mom closed on the old house on Friday, 29 August 2014 at 4:30PM. Phil, Gilda, and little Charlotte came up to spend the night and we all went straight over to start working. Jim and Phil tore out all the nasty carpeting and Gilda and I started priming the walls. Saturday was more priming and painting; we're using "Pure White" – no more baby

poop-colored walls! Gilda did all the cutting in; she is so careful and gets no primer or paint on any woodwork. Amazing.

Jim, Phil, and I installed hardwood flooring. Jim or Phil selected the pieces' patterns and made the cuts, I just rock'n'rolled, whacking in the pieces. Much slower going when I worked alone: selecting patterns, making cuts, and whacking 'em in place. Jim called me a "Flooring Goddess"! About the patterns, Dad, I refer to the actual designs on the flooring boards. Mom and I found a lovely flooring called *Delaware Bay Driftwood*. It looked like the Oregon Coast to us. Jim and I named every pattern so we could refer to them more easily. There's *Wave* and *Eye of Sauron* and *Eyelashes* and *Prairie Dog* and so many others. As I whacked boards into place, Jim would shout from another room, "When in doubt, use *Prairie Dog*!" Mom and I would grin whenever he did that. *Prairie Dog* was his favorite; I like *Wave* best, of course, you know me, anything oceany.

It is grueling work, physically, installing this flooring. My knees are completely black and blue (even with kneepads), and my hands are so swollen from the fitting and the whacking – it is all fun in a way, but physically, jeezus it's hard work. We marathoned for seven days. Starting before dawn, ending in the wee small hours of the morning. By the time Jim went back to California, we'd completely primed and painted every room, and the entire house had new flooring.

Dad, every project you ever did with us when we were little paid off for Mom this past week. We three did everything we could, and in my case, I can honestly say I did things I did not know I could ever do.
Love,
Alys

23 September 2014
Hiya Dad,
These days in September rollercoaster together, a mish-mash of flooring and painting, working at the old house. Today it is three months. Cris and I are going to a concert at LSS tonight. The first few concerts after you died were tough. Especially that very first one with *The Troubadours of Divine Bliss*, when they played "*Somewhere Over The Rainbow*" man, how I cried. Tonight, I expect something will make me cry. I'm prepared, I guess, to ride the rollercoaster that is today.
Love,
Alys

03 October 2014
Hiya Dad,
Recent days have been strange, busy, exhausting; I'm moving forward on the outside, but I'm sad inside. I'll try for some positive things here: remember my Reclaimed River Salvage Project and that I'm going to meet Rosanne Cash at her concert? I'll update you in both.

The concert was amazing, then they took us back to meet Rosanne Cash; she was kind, gracious, amazing. Her tour manager introduced us and gave her some details about why we were backstage. I mean, the other people backstage were two friends of hers and Jimmy Buffett's tour manager; we were definitely the "odd" group.

Her tour manager told her how I spent my birthday with you in the hospital and that you passed away three days later. She turned to me and said, "My mother died on my birthday, so I know exactly how you feel." Then she said we shouldn't talk anymore about sad things, and her tour manager took our photo: she put her arm around me and so I put my arm around her. I felt our hipbones touch.

Believe it or not, Dad: that's me, arm in arm with Rosanne Cash

Dad, she opened up my *Guitar Strang* pendant gift and put it on immediately I did not want to be pushy and ask for another photo with her wearing it! She could not have been nicer, more gracious, more kind. I know you and Johnny Cash enjoyed yourselves, watching me babble incoherently and seeing how wonderfully kind she was in response.

I have good days like Rosanne Cash and my Reclaimed River Salvage project. Thank you, Dad, for saving that old wooden frame for me, it made my piece possible. I also used your four little green plastic things as "feet." Mom and I have no idea what they were for originally, but we both are happy that I found a use for them. I took my finished fireplace screen over to the old house and took some photographs of it there: it looked great on the hearth. It's a success.

Dad, good days are still rare. I'd like to take a day for myself soon, to sit in my backyard, in my rocking chair, listening to the breeze move the branches of my trees (god, I love our home, our "cookie-cutter house" as Cris calls it. I love listening as the leaves murmur to me in voices from the past). Dad, do you remember all the trees we planted when I was little? Seems like everywhere we lived, we planted trees. I remember holding their trunks straight while you filled in the dirt around their roots. Yesterday, I planted a curly willow and a regular willow at the old house for Mom; she blew kisses with each tree.

We had a good day, Mom and I. We went to lunch at The Hamilton Restaurant. She loved it; said it was the best veggie burger she ever had, and she loved the desert, too (Hummingbird cake). We took two coconut macaroons to eat later. We had no plan to shop, but on a whim, we went

to Lowe's and I bought those willow trees. After I planted them, we sat in the screened porch and ate our macaroons. We had a good day, Dad, we truly did.
Love,
Alys

07 October 2014
Hiya Dad,
Well, I'm happy to report that we got Mom moved this past Saturday, as planned. It was a cold, windy, threatening-to-rain day, but we did it using my van and two flatbed trailers. Two loads on the trailers, Phil and Cris, moving all the big stuff. My van for all the smalls. I loaded and unloaded my van all day; quite tedious by the third load because Mom didn't really have enough boxes. She had all those ridiculous little plastic buckets; there must have been 100 of those buckets!

I'm so relieved Mom's moved; she is so much lighter, happier at the old house. I feel relieved, too, but, Dad, jeez I miss you and I miss John. I just miss you both. I'll keep busy, though, with the old house, with Mom, with art projects. I started two new paintings. I'm using your old canvases.
Love,
Alys

08 October 2014
Hiya Dad,
You never believed in any hocus-pocus; you must be kinda mad now! You're with Mom at the old house. You were there guiding my hand to turn that handle, helping us do everything, helping me with the flooring; everything. I felt your hand on my shoulder as I wrestled with your panty shelves; you put your hand there and whispered, *you can do this*. You are there. I'm so glad part of you is there, Dad.

You are free there. Maybe at the big house some part of you is hanging on, maybe there you are still a little frail and sad, but still you, with your know-it-all smile. Maybe that part of you is doing exactly what you wanted: never leaving *that* house. That's okay with me; I know *I'll* see you with Mom at the old house.

I love you.
Love,
Alys

23 December 2014
Hiya Dad,
Christmas is in two days, and I've been helping Mom with her decorations at the old house, putting up both our trees. How hard these traditions are, without you here. Mom's coming over to our house for our Christmas Feast, as will Aly and Evan. John will be with his friend Valentin's family in Rheims, France. Dad, he has been in Paris since yesterday. Amazing! He knows you were there sixty years ago. He wore your shoes to see the sights you saw, to stand where you stood. We traded text messages last night, because while he was seeing Paris for the first time, we all went on the train again, *The Polar Express*. One of the conductors played his guitar and led the train-car full of people in singing Christmas songs. Our favorite was *"Feliz Navidad."* I thought of you, Dad, because of your old Jose Feliciano record of ballads. I still have it; I still love it.

After the train ride, we went back to Mom's (new old) house and played Monopoly until after midnight; Charlotte won: she had *hotels* on Park Place and Boardwalk! I'll go over there again today. It's good for me to be up and about, after the pneumonia I had a couple weeks ago. I can't thank you enough for sitting with me for a little while that one day.

When I first felt your hand on mine, I thought it was Aly, stopping by after work. You and Aly are the only ones with always-warm hands. But after a few minutes, even with a fever, I knew it was you, not Aly. When I opened my eyes, there you were, sitting on the edge of my bed, just holding my hand and giving it a little squeeze every once in a while, exactly as I had done for you that awful final week in your hospital room. You sat with me for a while, then suddenly there was the scent of Grandmommy's *Emeraude*, and you squeezed my hand so tight, so hard, for about a minute, and then you both were gone. Right before I fell asleep, I remember being so happy that you and Grandmommy are together. Dad, you are getting more see-through, so I guess you might be letting go a little bit more. I'm glad I saw you, before these hard Christmas days. I just want to say to you, "I wanna wish you a Merry Christmas, I wanna wish you a Merry Christmas, I wanna wish you a Merry Christmas, from the bottom of my heart . . ."

Feliz Navidad, Dad, *Feliz Navidad*.
Love,
Alys

05 February 2015
Hiya Dad,
I have tried to allow some time to pass since last I wrote to you. I guess I was trying to let you rest, leave you alone a bit, and see how the days and weeks and months would feel. I think of *Casablanca*, and Sam singing, ". . . *a sigh is still a sigh, the fundamental things apply, as time goes by* . . . "

Christmas was hard, but we had a nice time all together; we all kept it as light and happy as possible, whilst missing both you and John. It helped to know he was in Paris, with friends. He sent photos of his feet in your shoes: outside the *Louvre* and in Reims. When he texted the photos, he simply wrote, "with Grandpa."

Films awards season is looming; Aly told me that she won't watch any this year. Always in the past she had you to talk to about the movies, the nominations, and the awards. She's bereft of you this year. We went to a movie, just the two of us, to honor your love of movies. Movies, Aly, and you; *as time goes by.*

Mom loves being home, in the old house. She wanders through each room, caressing the walls with her hand. She says that's all she wants, just to *be there*, forever. She says she doesn't want to leave, ever, even to go visit Jim or Phil. Both have asked her to visit them, but she refuses. She just doesn't want to leave the old house.

Well, Dad, I miss you.
Love,
Alys

17 June 2016
Hiya Dad,
Two years on, I wish memories didn't hurt so much. Good ones pull at your heartstrings, bad ones break you into pieces inside. I wish regrets could vanish into thin air, because you cannot DO anything about your regrets in the present. I wish there was some sort of real comfort for people dealing with loss and grief (fresh or old) but what is comfort? When does "time heal"? I thought keeping busy was the key; I don't know any more of there is a key. In my childhood, you were always busy: working in the yard, running road-races, running your twenty-five-mile training runs on weekends, doing projects around the house, and talking about music and books and movies like nobody's business. In the last couple years of your life, I never got used to you being quieter, just sitting

in a chair. We'd all get together for a holiday or birthday, and you'd occasionally join in the conversation, but mostly you were quiet. I can't get used to the quiet.

Two years ago today, you had that last massive stroke. I'll be with Mom today, and I'll be with her every day this week. I wish I could wave a magic wand and her hurt and sadness would vanish. Her health is more fragile; I don't know how much longer we'll have her with us. She loves us, but the biggest part of her just wants to be with you. Hard to see her constantly try to smile for us. Grief. In the past two years, I've learned that Grief never fades, it rocks you gently through the long dark nights, it shadows your movements in daytime's brightest sunshine, it drips through you and down you like sweat in the Summer, it cuts and whips you as sharply as Winter's icy winds, it falls crisp and dry like a blood-red leaf in Autumn falling to Earth, and it haunts you like a gray mist amidst the wondrous colors of Spring. Grief sneaks up on you suddenly and holds your hand constantly (I don't know how it does both at once, but it does). You live with Grief like a person; you have a relationship with Grief. You sit at the table with Grief, you watch TV with Grief, you argue, you fight, you love, you turn to Grief for comfort. Grief is both your adversary and your best friend. It stops you in your tracks and it pulls you forward.
We are never alone.
Grief is always there.
I miss you, Dad.
Love,
Alys

Author's Notes: John came home from Germany in August of 2016, and Aly and Evan were married on my dad's birthday that year. My mother was completely happy those two days; having John home safe meant the world to her, and she loved that we were all together for Aly's wedding. We all felt my dad's presence fully those bittersweet days. Then, as life will do, it took a turn. Starting in March of 2017, I spent every day with my Mom as her health failed. By May she had been in and out of the hospital for the last time, and June was simply a horrible long hard goodbye. My tiny sweet mom passed away in July. As she had requested, we placed her ashes in the backyard of her beloved house, at the base of two new trees that we planted especially for her. That summer day, we all wondered silently, *What will become of this beloved house now?* Mom and Jim had purchased the house with a life estate to Jim, so our mom's death meant it was now Jim's alone, and we all knew it would have to be sold. Being the one here, it fell to me to empty Mom's house, preparing it for an inevitable sale. I spent weeks and weeks sorting, packing, going through my parents' belongings, their lifetimes emotionally sorted *via* my new mantra, *keep, sell, donate, trash, keep, sell, donate, trash.*

Then, life took another strange turn; more hocus-pocus. My husband and I would buy the house from Jim. Suddenly, overlapping the emptying of my mother's house, I was also sorting, packing, emptying *our* home of eighteen years. Our lifetimes sorted *via* that mantra, *keep, sell, donate, trash, keep, sell, donate, trash.*

I left behind almost everything I had planted. My trees, wisteria, lilac, magnolia, and my rose garden. I moved only two roses (out of twenty-five), one juniper, and my rock garden. Moving our belongings took weeks; while my husband was at work, I moved stuff one van-load at a time, just as I had moved most of my mother's belongings three short years ago. I moved more boxes than I could count (but no ridiculous little baskets, thank god!). Pieces of furniture that I didn't think I could lift, somehow I lifted them into/out of my van and into the old house. I felt my father's hand on my shoulder and heard his voice in my ear: *you can do this*. In early October, my husband and I moved the last of our largest items on flatbed trailers, just as he and Phil had moved my mother's stuff three short years before. When we closed in mid-October, life started in earnest at our new old house, but it took me a long time to unpack all our boxes and arrange our furniture. I held up paintings against walls and moved the furniture around in every room; each piece I moved six, seven, eight times or more. Automatically, I'd turn to ask my mom what she thought of this or that arrangement. I felt her presence; she told me she loves everything I've done to make the house Cris' and mine. As I walk on *Wave* and *Eye of Sauron* and *Eyelashes* and *Prairie Dog* and the others, I grin remembering Jim shouting, "When in doubt, use *Prairie Dog*!" Mom grins with me.

One more hocus-pocus. Putting our own house on the market during one of the coldest Indiana winters in recent history was scary; what if no offer came? We feared we'd be paying two mortgages through Spring.

Then, on my mother's birthday, 02 January 2018, a day I spent weeping and wishing I could hug her one more time, well that day the right people went to see our house; they made an offer the next day. I believe Mom led them there on her birthday; it was a hocus-pocus cosmic hug from her. I love her so much. I miss her so much. I know she's happy we're here, and I love being here, but *happy* just isn't *my* word yet.

We sleep now in the bedroom that was long ago my parents' bedroom and so recently my mother's bedroom. Our bed's headboard rests along the same wall that framed the headboard of my parents' bed, my mother's bed. When I walk into that room, I try not to see my mother as she was when I returned with the nectarines on that last sad day. I'll get better about that, someday. In the meantime, I walk through this house, these beloved rooms, as my mother did, running my hand along the walls, caressing them; remembering.

Yes, *happy* might not yet be my word, but I'll get there. When I put up our Christmas tree and decorated it with our family ornaments, my mom was there at my side: I heard her sweet laugh and saw her joyous smile. Aly and Evan, John and Lily, Phil and Gilda and Charlotte all gathered here on New Year's Eve. Aly and Cris made Macedonian *komet* and *tatlia* just like my Baba and my mom used to make. We all played monopoly 'til way past midnight, and we talked about movies and books and music.

I saw my mom in the kitchen, smiling at us.

No one's ever really gone.

My mom and my dad are happy that this house will be where our kids always come home for holiday meals and birthday celebrations. They're happy it will be where our grandchildren come to visit, where we'll talk music and books and movies with them, where we'll play Monopoly 'til way past midnight when our grandchildren spend the night. I feel my father and my mother everywhere here.

I never want to leave this house.

Somewhere Over The Rainbow

Annie Oberman

Blue.

Maren Thornbury

He walked in with a metal bat. It was blue and dented and broken, just like his eyes. They held so much pain and I could see cracks and a million scars in their reflection. He dragged the bat behind him, but he was not defeated. He was angry. He was furious. He had the rawest anger I had ever seen. The man stood there with his cracked eyes and his broken body, his wrist covered in bruises, his watch bent and shattered. But still visible, the numbers still there like they always will be. The man had one week left. He stared at me with his shattered dazzling blue eyes, full of so much hatred. And all I could do was look back. A contest of some sort resumed, who would break first? It felt like hours we stood there, locked in each other's gaze. Then everything exploded like a bomb that had been waiting for years to go off. He raised his bat and he hit the grandfather clock next to him, he beat it until it was nothing but splintered wood and glass. I stood there, I took it. And then he hit the clocks on the wall. He shattered the display cases and destroyed the gold and silver and metal watches that lay in a sparkling line. I stood there and watched him. I watched as he took his bat to the walls, to the floor, to the windows and the door. He screamed as he killed it; wet, angry, tears streaming down his cheeks. I remember it like it happened yesterday, how could I have ever forgotten? How could I have forgotten everything he shouted at the Time he was destroying?

"You aren't real!" He screamed until his throat was raw.

"You were never real!"

A solid gold pocket watch explodes into a million pieces.

"You don't own me!"

An alarm clock thrown at the window, glass cuts his cheek.

"We don't owe you nothing! You don't matter! You don't control me or anyone or anything!"

He stopped, surrounded by his pain. Surrounded by darkness. And he whispered this time. The bat hung limply at his side and blood traced his face.

"My entire life... I believed in you, I believed in it all. I put all my faith on this system. I trusted it, I accepted it. I knew we didn't last forever... I knew you were meant to be. And I believed this concept was freeing..."

His eyes were shimmering now. Like waves in the ocean. He dropped the blue bat on the glass shards surrounding him. They crunched beneath its weight. His voice rose once more, it boomed and echoed off the walls. And I saw that he was not broken, he was the strongest man I'd ever meet.

"But I reject that! I reject you and all your bullshit! You are not free! You cannot float! You are fleeting! You can't fly away. For we have clipped your wings. And you are not our prison, we are yours. You are the bird, and we are the cage that holds you. You think you are the freedom! But we are your oppression! You have fooled all of mankind into thinking that we need you. That you trapped us. That you define us... but we define you. We trap you. Time would not exist without us, without our belief in you!"

He stood to his feet, he screamed at the debris on the floor. At Time.

"But I reJECT YOU! I will NEVER BELIEVE IN YOU AGAIN! You took EVERYTHING! This THING on my wrist doesn't control me or anyone, I won't let it. This will happen on my own terms, I die on my OWN TERMS! Not yours. Never yours. I won't be consumed by you again. You are, Time is, and always will be an allusion. A hallucination. A mirage. This is real. I am real. You were never real. You are only as real as we allow you to be. And I won't allow you to be real to me anymore."

He fell to his knees, he looked at me again. His eyes were no longer broken and scarred, they were flaming. They were alive. I felt tears cutting my cheeks then, the glass shards in my palm from the clock I had crushed dripped blood on the carpet. His new eyes pierced me like a spear.

And one last thing escaped his cracked lips, "You will never be real."

And then he looked to his wrist, stitched with all the scars and bruises of his past. He lifted a shaking hand....

He took the watch off.

The numbers frozen, the time stuck in place.

He just took it off.

I watched it fall in slow motion and the sound of it hitting the ground was deafening. He looked at me, and I looked at him. Just a young boy who wouldn't even remember his act. He stood up. Though the man would leave me silently, the realization he brought would not reach me until this moment. Nothing was ever real. Time was never real. I let It control me, I allowed this concept of time to consume my every waking moment. And it was never real. Never. I made it real. I made it a part of me. When the whole time, the whole time I could have just taken it off. I could have just taken it off.

When I open my eyes the scene is the same. People are screaming. The plane is plummeting to the ground. I am silent and still, staring at the watch on my wrist. There are 60 seconds left. With a sigh I close my eyes once more and place a tender hand over the face of the clock. I think back to all those years ago, the things that man screamed in my father's store. I use his rage to fuel my own, and with a tiny click. My numbers stop and the green interface falls into the chaos of the airborne plane. Tears stream down my face, I was an idiot. I look out the window and the world is on fire, or maybe it's just the engine. I let out a soft chuckle, close my eyes, and wait. My life, and everything I ever did with it, was all a waste of Time anyway.

And then I am gone.

Going Green Gone Bad

Gail Geisler
Honorable Mention, Prose Category

It was all my sister's fault, I told her later. If it hadn't been for her none of it would have happened….

I headed out the door to lunch, a thousand thoughts racing through my head. I was still reeling from finding out that my sister just had an emergency quadruple bypass. She looked bad when I saw her, pale, weak, a shadow of herself, grey skin on the white hospital pillow. And not that old when it happened – she's younger than me. Must be genetic, since we lost my dad so young to a heart attack. It all just scared the crap out of me.

But what a nice truck, I thought, as I unlocked and opened the door. Brand new, loaded, leather, sun roof, black and shiny as hell except the road dust on the back end from a recent trip to a job site. *I earned this*, I thought as I climbed in. Never had such a nice vehicle and it made me smile when I got a whiff of that new car smell. Sitting up high, looking out over the hood, and feeling like a king in my new king cab. OK – so a quick trip to the hardware store to pick up some paint, grab some lunch, wash my new truck, then back to our small construction office. I got this, as long as I hurry. And I can eat in the car wash.

I ran into Ace Hardware, grabbed the largest can of green spray paint I could find and laid it on the floor behind the driver's seat. Then I headed to the drive through at McDonald's. I was about to order my usual Big Mac and large fries, when my sister's face in the hospital popped back into my head. OK, OK, so maybe I should try a healthy green salad. First time ever. Sounds like an oxymoron doesn't it? Who goes to McDonald's for a salad?

I pulled into the car wash, paid, and followed the gestures of the high school kid who thought he needed to direct me onto the track. Once the truck started moving, I opened the salad and added the dressing. How do you even eat this crap? I slid my seat back to fit the salad container on my lap between my belly and the steering wheel. That's when things went very, very, wrong.

There was a small explosion, and in the time that it took for me to register what it was, my car started filling up with green spray paint. There's a lot of paint under a lot of pressure in a spray can. When it gets punctured, it comes out. *No, no, NO! Not in my new truck.* I whipped the salad off my lap and tried to open the door. But the truck was moving, something was blocking the way, and water blasted in. I slammed the door, but then I couldn't breathe. The entire cab was filling up with a green mist and I started to cough.

I opened the windows and got slapped in the face with those heavy wet octopus straps of dirty felt that are supposed to wipe off your car. I gasped for air and got slapped again. I rolled up the window. So much paint in that damn can! Why did I buy the big one? I couldn't breathe, paint filling the cab with green aerosol gas and coating everything inside. Again I tried to open the window, this time to be hit by a forceful spray of rinse water. Like someone throwing a bucket of water in my face. Panicked and coughing, I closed it again. And so it went. The last time I opened the window, dry air blasted my face so hard I felt my cheeks flapping, matching the way the wipers chattered on the glass.

When my truck was finally released from the conveyor, I jumped out. I tried to breathe and collect myself. *What just happened?* My truck was trashed, the beautiful white leather interior covered in green paint, slimy salad, and soapy water. And so was I. *Shit.* Confused, dazed, and maybe affected by the fumes, I slowly slid back in. I drove back to the office with all the windows open, leaning my head out the driver's window to see where I was going, vaguely aware of the wind blasting my hair and the shocked looks from the other drivers.

Back at the office parking lot, I looked in the center mirror and blinked back at myself. The only pale skin that remained was on my eyelids. My hair was green, stiff, and frozen at a bizarre angle, thanks to the wind and the paint. Lettuce and veggies were stuccoed to my hair and chest.

The truck interior was trashed. My new car smell had been replaced by a searing paint smell with maybe a hint of bacon buttermilk ranch....

Yep, if it hadn't been for my sister and the damn green salad, none of it would have happened. No heart surgery, no healthy salad, no reason to slide the seat back to eat it. It was definitely all her fault.

Bannerman
Rachel Cox

There he is!
The light-bringer hope-weaver
with the strong chin and
Fire in his eyes

Look how he waves that banner
and carries our Dreams
on those broad shoulders

Shame he's a liar.

In The Now
DeMaris Gaunt

Four Kitchen Utensils I Would Love to Have
Cynthia Baker

A slotted spoon for removing the hubris from those in power.

A spritzer to add a light coat of well-being on the over those who feel over-worked, under-appreciated, super-stressed, or un-loved.

An infuser of love, peace, and empathy that could be dunked into ugly family disputes, violent protests, and wars.

A spatula that could lift me up, very gently, very softly, from my relaxed, done with yoga, *savasana* pose and smoothly transport me, sliding me, ever so quietly, from the spatula to my bed at home for a good night's sleep.

Mirror

DeMaris Gaunt
Second Prize, Song Lyric/Poetry Category

To prove
that I'm racist
my daughter
asks me
questions
like would you
rather adopt
a white child
or a black one
and I say
I'm not raising
any more kids
and she asks
if I'd feel
more comfortable
in a room
full
of white people
or black
and my answer
is wrong
true
complicated
and we sit
in silence
for a while
sipping coffee
thinking of

more questions
that no one
wants to answer
so she can get an A
on her paper
that's going to
be a mirror
no one wants
to look into.

Talking to Ghosts

Ellen Santasiero

A painting on a wall is an attitude ... It says this is the way it is according to a given sensibility ... this is a way of viewing what is to be viewed. – Richard Diebenkorn

It's one week after 9/11, and you're on the phone with United, trying to get a flight home to the west coast from New York. You're at your parents' house upstate, leaning against the kitchen door frame, looking into the living room where your father watches the news.

"I'm still checking, ma'am," United says.

In the kitchen behind you, your mother puts together a salad. You hear the newsman interview people who suggest we might respond to the attack with love and nonviolence.

Your father bats towards the screen. "Buncha nuts."

On the wall in the dining room, you see a pen and ink drawing of a chickadee you did for him for Father's Day one year. In the living room beyond his chair hangs your lithograph of the lake in winter. Above his bureau in the bedroom is the calligraphy on yellow parchment of the serenity prayer that you made for him when you were fourteen. You spend several minutes on hold, watching the TV screen, and silently agreeing with the pacifists.

Friends of your parents come to dinner. Your father says responding to the terrorists with love and peace is ridiculous. Foolish.

"Let me tell you something about those people, they'll do anything to get what we have. They're thieves."

All the guests agree, and so you don't respond. You give the chicken breast on your plate a stab.

How many times have you stood before your lecturing father, speechless?

How many opinions did he hand down to you at the kitchen table, starting when you were very young? You were nine, ten, eleven, just an observing consciousness, just a couple of breath's weight to his heavy step, his deeply creased brow, the blade of his white collar pressed against the back of his ruddy neck, listening, listening to him talk at you about Right and Wrong.

Shaking his finger at you for emphasis, he leaned forward in his chair, leaned back, the muscles in his face tensing and relaxing. A fly worried incessantly at the window sill. He slapped the table, drove his index finger straight down on the Formica during the important part, the lazy lid over his right eye sliding fully open. You were not asked to respond. When he was done, he excused you, and you, your head spinning a little, found an old mayonnaise jar and went to catch tadpoles in the brook next to the house.

About having a strong parent who rarely asks you to speak, think: this is what it must be like to not exist. ... *sew the leg to the collar,* said the poet Judy Ruiz. *Put the garment on. Sew the mouth shut.* The longer you lived with him, the more invisible you became. You stopped speaking, the muscle atrophied. But you did exist. You existed in some kind of limbo, some kind of liminal space. And like other liminal beings, you became haunted, and in danger of haunting.

You help your mother with the dishes, and then bid the guests good night, and go to bed. As you get ready to sleep on the couch in your father's home office, you notice the artifacts that surround you: awards and certificates from New York University and the National Cash Register Company, a citation from 1945 framed in black, praising your father for his sniper abilities in Italy, his bronze star, his purple heart.

As you lay in the dark, you think about your father's conviction about using military force, and yours about the power of nonviolence. He says our military is the reason we have a good life. You know how real this relationship is for him, as real as the weight of the M-1 he hefted through the Po Valley, as real as the time it took him to figure out how to shift from a life of daily fear and dread to one of hope and expectation back at home. You understand this in your mind only; you admit you take this freedom for granted. You have no practical experience with either war or nonviolence, but a question twitches inside of you, like a phantom limb, or a vestigial flipper: *Is war the only way?* You turn, try to get comfortable.

From the small, single bed, you notice the moon. It shines clear and bright through the black woods, but looks stuck in the tangled tree branches. You feel like a child again, as you often do in his house. Nothing you say can compare to his memory of dragging his friend Tex – leg blown off –

to safety, or to the months he spent living in cold camps watching other buddies die, all the while believing that he was fighting to help preserve goodness in the world. You can't stand up to Riva Ridge. You are dwarfed by Mt. Belvedere. Be humbled by the star. Kneel before the heart.

You remember holding up a charcoal gesture drawing you did of your boyfriend, the one where he's sitting on a couch with his left leg foreshortened, so your father could see. The rice paper made shushing sounds as you handled it.

"He looks like he was in a car accident," said your father, rapping his empty water glass on the table.

You were home from college showing your parents the art you made in school. About art, you and your father's tastes diverge. In the living room, he hung a realistic painting of a mountain with a lick of white frosting on its peak. You like Ocean Park #27 by Richard Diebenkorn, the one where the blue goes off the right side of the canvas and the yellow off the upper left.

You feel something shut down in your gut and you put the charcoal drawing and the other pieces back in the black portfolio he bought you. You feel shut down even as you feel grateful to him for the portfolio, and the charcoal, and the rice paper.

You forget to take your prescription and you get up to find the orange vial in your suitcase. On top of your clothes you see a large black and white photograph of the art critic Clement Greenberg. The photo is in a program from an art exhibit you recently attended.
In graduate school, you became obsessed with Greenberg and his once-famous 1939 essay, *Avant Garde and Kitsch*. You fell in love with the complete confidence of Greenberg's voice. "...folk art is not Athene, and it's Athene whom we want: formal culture with its infinity of aspects, its luxuriance, its large comprehension." His prose harbored no allusion, no innuendo; nothing lurked or smoldered in Greenberg's prose. As the imperious, logical sentences marched to their inevitable conclusions, you felt the urge to go change into something crisp and navy blue. Because you wanted your own writing to sound more authoritative, you studied his word choices –" must," "simply," "no accident" – and noted the breadth of his references: Picasso, Yeats, Dwight MacDonald, Aristotle, Repin, Mallarme, Gottfried Benn. Your mind fizzed.

For months, you kept the essay on a corner of your desk. You made it your bearing tree, the thing you used to test other writers on aesthetics. It seemed larger than an essay, it promised answers. What does Greenberg say? What would Greenberg say? For a time, you let these questions direct everything you read and wrote.

You remember that in the exhibit of Greenberg's art collection, there were large text panels on the gallery walls screened with Greenberg's opinions. It occurs to you that, when you were growing up, it was as if there were text panels on the walls of your house emblazoned with your father's opinions.

In the living room: "When a young man takes you out on a date, he should treat you to a nice dinner."

Above the fish tank: "Protesting the government is wrong."

And above your bed: "Don't invest in insurance annuities."

In the photograph in the exhibit program, Greenberg stares directly at the camera, unsmiling. He resembles your father (eyelids, schnoz), and there are other minor similarities – they were both New Yorkers, both children of European immigrant stock – but it is the authoritative stance, the certainty about their opinions, their power to name things for you, that makes you blur them in your mind. You realize, staring at the photograph, that even though you've moved far, far away from your father, you've been entertaining his spirit for years through an art critic who looks and sounds like him.

You get back in bed, shiver under the covers, and realize that it isn't just Greenberg. You've always been drawn to highly opinionated and well-spoken men. You weep at the sound of a southern preacher even though you've never been to the South and were raised Catholic. In your twenties you found a confident and eloquent boyfriend who showed little interest in your life. *You stood before him, speechless.* After seven months with this boyfriend, you developed a stutter. It occurred to you, for the first time, in that small office bed, that perhaps this was not solely his fault.

The next morning, you get up, and in the light see another artifact in your father's office: the paperweight you made for him when you were a kid. It's a rock with pasted-on green and blue felt letters spelling "Dad." You pick it up, enjoy the weight of it in your hand. Even though you don't know how to defend your idea about peace, especially against the clear and weighty facts of your father's soldier's life, you know that you have to speak. You must say something. You tell yourself: *Just say one thing.*

The brown wooden stairs creak and pop as you climb them to the kitchen where your parents are drinking coffee. You choose a cup, fill it, and sit down. The yellow cloth napkins are still on the table from the night before. Your mother's blue sweater vest matches her blue eyes; she smiles at you. Your father, dressed in gray sweats, clears his throat loudly, and wipes his mouth with a small square of paper towel.

"How did you sleep down there?"

After you answer, you sit back with one arm crossed over your stomach, play with the yellow napkin, and try to think.

You smooth the napkin.

You turn to your father and say your one thing: "I felt angry when you were ridiculing the pacifists on the news last night."

The house does not come crashing down.

And then, after the lecture about America, the one you have heard all your life, blasts from the engine of your father's mouth, an extraordinary thing happens. He asks you a question.

So what would this love and peace look like? That's what he asked you.

You have no answer. You haven't even eaten breakfast, and it's been a full day for you already. The conversation sputters, comes to a halt. But you eat heartily, and feel the sun on your face later when you sit on the porch.

Later, much later, remembering this question in a place of quiet, a piece of art comes to mind: a green and gold copper bas relief you saw in Ireland that shows several pairs of faces, side by side, each sharing an eye with the face next to it. Each face is complete in and of itself, yet each face's right or left eye also belongs to the face next to it. And so on down the line of faces. They are separate and together at the same time. Each would be limited without the other. No doubt, each is limited with the other, too, but it's this separate-and-together theme, this suggestion of empathy that interests you.

Next time you talk to him, you'll say, "That's what my idea of love and peace would look like, Dad."

But wait, you've got the paperweight, too. Maybe you should have brought that paperweight upstairs that morning, and said: "Here, Dad, here is a paperweight I made for you. Remember? See how it contains both of us? See how I made it, and see how you keep it? What part of this rock is not me, or you, or the two of us, together?"

These questions are for another day, if it ever comes. Right now, you just have to remember that you can talk to ghosts, and it doesn't really make a difference whether they listen or not. It's the talking to those who scare you that matters, because talking to them will eventually make them go away.

Disappearing Nickel Plate Blues

Steve VandeWater
(song lyric)

The Nickel Plate's gone off the track, and brother she ain't comin' back
When politicians' plans have been approved.
The once proud line's in disrepair
And though folks just don't seem to care
They'll miss her when her rails have been removed

The rusted rails and ties that bind, of yesteryear they do remind
When trains were vital to economy.
But nowadays when railroads fail
We turn the lines to biking trail
And trains are something people rarely see.

John Henry and Ol' Casey Jones are prob'ly rattlin' in their bones
And spinning like a cyclone in their graves.
Their legacies will die out soon
Remembered only in a tune
Because the local railroads can't be saved

Our train is local history, but those in charge can't seem to see
The railroad links us to our homegrown ways.
They'd rather see more hiking trails
Than wooden ties and rusty rails
That link us to the fabled "Good Ole Days"

The Nickel Plate is one such line, her glory days are far behind
In recent times to catch a glimpse was rare.
But even though she seldom ran
Year after year the folks would plan
To climb aboard and ride her to the Fair.

And once the train is dead and gone, no more for folks to ride upon
To see a train they'll go to a museum.
Those trains won't move or sound the horn
Just sit there, idle and forlorn
But that's the only way we'll get to see 'em

John Henry and Ol' Casey Jones are prob'ly rattlin' in their bones
And spinnin' like a cyclone in their graves.

Their legends too will die out soon
Remembered only in a tune
Because a local railroad wasn't saved

#SaveTheTrain
Alys Caviness-Gober

Windswept
W. B. Cornwell

It was in my youth, when I was easily frightened
by heavy rain, lightning and wind.

Blackened angry skies overhead
would always fill me with dread.

Once when the sky turned gray
I worried for someone far away.

Although at the time we were miles apart
I could not ease my worried heart.

As the weather raged on and on
with a furry ever so fiercely strong.

At home I could not ignore the eerie chill
of the happenings far away in Noblesville.

The winds collided and rain poured
a tornado formed and it roared.

It came and tore through the place
sparring all, so again I seen my loved one's face.

My Secret Addiction
Anonymous (a friend of Bill W.)

God grant me the serenity to accept the things I cannot change, Courage to change the things I can, and the Wisdom to know the difference. – from a prayer by Reinhold Niebuhr

It all started when I young. Really young. Too young to know better, I guess. My dad told me once that I asked him about it; his response was basically a brush-off. I don't know about you, but a brush-off always makes me want whatever it is even more. My dad's cavalier attitude is at least partly to blame for my secret addiction.

I hid it pretty well for most of my childhood. Well, that was kinda someone else's fault, too. I had an older sister who controlled my life with mental and physical bullying. I mean, she was *mean-girl* personified. Being only one year older than me, there wasn't really a time in my early childhood that she wasn't just there, bossing, controlling, manipulating my emotions, punching, scratching, threatening to kill me . . . yikes, I digress into the abyss of scary memories; I'm a little PTSD about all that stuff. But yeah, back then, the beginning of my instinct to keep my addiction a secret was totally her fault. Just so you know: taking the above prayer to heart, I made a change and cut her out of my life completely. I don't admit to people that I have a sister. Anyone who knew us growing up, well, they know I refer to her as *my former sister*, if I even refer to her at all.

I tried once, when I was in my late 20s/early 30s, to set myself free, to conquer my addiction. I set myself on a path of embracing other things so fully that my life did not have room for my addiction. You can probably guess how *that* turned out, right? Failure!

Actually, to be fair, I didn't so much fail as I was totally undermined by someone else. *That* guy was also a manipulative brutal abuser and really did a number on my efforts to conquer my addiction. I mean, when someone threatens you, blames you for every little thing, burns your belongings, chokes you, punches you, breaks your teeth – wait, there I go again down into the PTSD abyss – let's just say makes your life a living HELL every moment, well, it's almost impossible *not* to retreat into your old comfort-zone habits, right? (Even if your old comfort-zone habits ain't exactly healthy.) Really, man, me falling off the wagon back then was totally *his* fault, not mine.

At some point, I guess it was about five years ago when I turned 50, I just gave up and gave in 100% to my addiction. I mean, it is just too hard to stop, you know? And really, who does it hurt? Also, it's *my* business, right? Why can't people just leave me alone?? I mean, you know this **IS** America, after all, and I have the right to privacy and pursuit of happiness and all that shit, right? So fuck off, World, I say! Ha! Anyway, about five or six years ago, yep, I just gave up trying.

Well, I didn't really "give up." I mean, it's not like I lacked some internal moral characteristic or willpower or anything like that – in fact, you know what? It was really just a simple matter of timing. Yeah, time is basically to blame, if the truth be told. I mean, everyone goes through some kind of "issues" when they hit that half-century mark, right? Some people do really stupid stuff, like have affairs or get divorced or run off to a commune to find themselves (whatever the Hell *that* means) or buy little red sports cars or expensive boats or motorcycles. I mean, it ain't called *having a mid-life crisis* for nothing, right? That shit just happens when you reach a certain age, you know, that's proven fact.

So, yeah, it's definitely not *my* fault.

Prayer Circle
Spike Wilson

Morning Bell

The bell sounds
and the world smiles.
Beings, called to wakefulness,
begin the day.

Birds claim the sky.
Grass dances, flowers reach.
Hidden creatures stir beneath the
ground.
Living things walk to greet one
another.

The bell sounds.
Winds sweep healing
prayers down the mountainside.
Clouds move across the sky.

Rising with the sun,
awareness also dawns.
Reborn in each moment,
silent witnesses attend
to the needs of all beings.

Because You Draw Breath

When the heart cries out,
  who will hear
  if even you do not understand?
Who will account for the silent
injustices,
  unseen wounds,
  nightmares unuttered long after
the sleeper awakes?

Beloved, give voice to your
anguish,
  your rage, your shame.
Call upon me

to find the healing balm
for hands wounded by a violent
world.

This is my greatest wish for you,
A prayer uttered with every
breath,
Fervent, set to each footstep of
my life.

But I am neither mother nor
father to you.
I am no savior, no god, no hero,
no teacher.

I know your pain because it
reflects my own.
I am helpless in its wake, though
I call
upon all that I know
upon every power
upon every god and prophet and
healer.

I only have this to give you:
That the same wind blows cold
in every desolate heart.
My blood runs the same when
it reddens the earth.

Maybe this is hope,
when we meet in our suffering,
when the only prayer I know to
be true
is uttered between silences so
deeply known:
"I am here. Because you draw
breath, I love you."

I Begin

I am sorry I took so long to find
you,
You who were always there.
The pain of a lifetime turned my
eyes away.
I did not know you arrived
before memory.
You smile at my blindness,
and with that same smile
healed it utterly.

There is so much to do.
Dawn approaches.
Birds are shadows against the
rising sun.
The world is once again awake.
I am awake with it.
I breathe.
I begin.

Returning

In stillness, each breath becomes
music.
In silence, each sound eternity
echoed and reflected.
You are the notes and the silence
between them,
pauses of expectation and hope.

Returning home with each
moment,
Enwrapped in your warmth,
I reach out to all living things.
May each moment of my life
benefit them!

Soothe through my hands those
who sleep restlessly.
Make my arms strong, so I may
pull beings from suffering.

Transform my tears into
nourishing drink,
my blood into a river by which
things grow.
Awaken me to the sounds of the
world's cries,
Sweep clean and open my heart,
Make it a shelter for the poorest
ones.

Make my eyes reflections
through which they may
see their true selves
their endless capacities
the wisdom and love we all share
if we would only look.

Remake me in each moment
to be father and mother,
child and teacher,
spouse, monk, servant, mirror,
all permutations
to fulfill their needs.

Rebuild this temple in each
moment
until it is no longer needed.
Then return it
to a secret place where
flowers bear silent witness.

Forgotten by all but you,
purify me this last time.
Dissolve me utterly
to become nourishment
for all the precious things that
move under the earth.

Evening Bell

The bell sounds
and all beings are called home.

The sky empties.
The warm earth
prepares for tomorrow.

The bell sounds
as the moon rises.
There is still so much to do.
But rest now, precious ones.
The sky watches over you.
We will share tomorrow.

2018 The Polk Street Review Prizes

Award of Merit (Best in Book)
Vibrations in VII by Celeste Williams

Prose Category:

Tie for *First Prize*:
The Great State of Canada by Jenny Kalahar
House of Dreams by Vivian Belle

Second Prize:
Blood Brothers by Jerry Dreesen

Tie for *Third Prize*:
Home Invasion by Nicole Amsler
The Smoking and Joking Santa by Mark Wilkinson

Honorable Mentions:
Going Green Gone Bad by Gail Geisler
Jimmy and the Stingray Summer by Greg Richards

Poetry/Song Lyrics:

First Prize:
The Banned Book by Susan Hoskins Miller

Second Prize:
Mirror by DeMaris Gaunt

Third Prize:
A Week in The Life Of... by Jo Mader

Honorable Mentions:
(How) To Kill a Mockingbird or Two Men and a Truck
    by Steve VandeWater
Spooky Town by Jean Roberts

Images Category:

First Prize:
Cabin in the Woods by Jerry Dreesen

Tie for *Second Prize*:
Farmers Market Flowers: Perspective
   by Kathryn Anderson
Magic Mushroom by Gail Geisler

Tie for *Third Prize*:
A Serengeti Sunrise in Central Indiana
   by Sam Watermeier
Praying by Annie Oberman

***Honorable Mentions*:**
The Spirit Within by Kristina Oliver
Tenacity by Cynthia Baker

Three *Special Awards:*

Sandra (Sandy) Stewart is a longtime submitter to TPSR, and the award recognizes Sandy for always submitting poetry and prose filled with great imagination, and for her enthusiasm and support for TPSR and LSS in general.

Maren Thornbury receives the award as our youngest submitter; we are impressed with, and want to encourage, her overall talent.

 Al Geisler receives the award because his submissions are   both creative fits to this year's theme and his prose submission is a first-attempt at writing.

Biographies

Kathryn Anderson currently resides in Noblesville with her husband, dog, and two cats. Kathryn has been a part of the Noblesville community for over twenty years. In her free time, Kathryn enjoys journaling, reading, photography, hiking, and walking her dog.

Anonymous (*A friend of Bill W.*) is, well, anonymous.

Cynthia Anne Baker has lived in Noblesville, Indiana for almost 20 years. She's never lived for so long in one place, in one home. Journaling and writing have always been important to her health and wellness. Cynthia is very thankful for the work and talents of so many who give TPSR and its gifts to the Noblesville community.

Tim A. Baker has lived in Noblesville for almost twenty years. He enjoys writing, playing guitar, and spending time with his family.

Arlene Barker is originally from the Chicago area, and moved to Hamilton County in 1973. She taught in Hamilton Southeastern Schools for many years where she wrote student plays about local history. After retiring from teaching and then twelve years at Conner Prairie, she became active with the local writing community through the Indianapolis Writing Center. She enjoys monthly meetings with a writing critique group for encouragement and to share thoughts and words. Besides writing, Arlene enjoys reading, gardening, yoga, and traveling to see her children and grandchildren. She lives in a house in the woods with her husband, Peter, and their dog, Penny.

Vivian Belle has lived in Noblesville for over forty years. Vivian enjoys writing in her leisure time. She's never submitted anything for publication prior to submitting to this edition of *The Polk Street Review*.

Alys Caviness-Gober is a disabled artist, writer, nonprofit volunteer, and is a Juried Artist member (in photography and 2D art) in the *Hamilton County Artists' Association* (HCAA). Before her health issues worsened, Alys was working on a PhD in Applied Linguistics and taught Anthropology, Women's Studies, and ESL at Ball State University. Alys is a co-founder of and Secretary for *Logan Street Sanctuary, Inc.* (LSS), and publisher/editor at *Logan Street Sanctuary Press*. Along with Sarah E. Morin, she co-founded *NICE* (*Noblesville Interdisciplinary Creativity Expo*). Alys and her husband Cris live in Noblesville, where they raised their two children.

John Caviness grew up in Noblesville. He received his BA in Foreign Languages (German Studies) and is in his final semester of Grad School at Ball State University's *Center for Communication and Information Sciences*.

Radka Caviness (02 January 1939 – 08 July 2017) lived in Noblesville for forty-two years. She and her late husband Jim raised their children in New York, Washington, Oregon, California, Georgia, and Indiana.

W. B. (William Benjamin) Cornwell is an award-winning poet and one half of the writing team known as *Storm Sandlin*. In 2016, he and his cousin, A. N. Williams, co-ran the campaign for Elwood Indiana's *Poetry Month*. He is also a charter member of *The Write Idea*.

Rachel Cox is a lifelong resident of Noblesville, and is currently studying Writing and Literacy at Indiana University-Purdue University Indianapolis (IUPUI). After graduation she plans to go into the publishing business. Along with a general love of the bizarre and esoteric, she enjoys strong black tea and distrusts anyone who doesn't like cats.

Reina DeCapua is married to Matthew, is a mother of two, and currently resides in Carmel, IN. Reina wrote her first poem in 1993 and didn't write again until 2014. Her favorite place is being in nature: in a valley, on a mountain, in a field of flowers, or at the beach. Reina works professionally as an Electrical Engineer.

DeMaris Gaunt is a poet and artist who has lived in Hamilton County for eleven years. She served on the Fishers Art Council for two years and has an affinity for anything unusual and original. She spends as much time as she can adventuring outdoors and is currently building her forever home in Nashville Indiana. If she could tell you anything, she would tell you to quit worrying about finding happiness. Happiness is overrated. Find something you love and let it kill you. It will be much more satisfying and meaningful.

Al Geisler's family has lived in Noblesville since 1987. His families is from Michigan. Al's brother, Dave, and he were senior lifeguards on the South Haven public beach. You might sometime see Al around Noblesville – he's the guy wearing the *Got Fish?* hat.

Gail Geisler grew up in Michigan, went to Michigan State, got hired by Lilly and moved to Noblesville in 1987. She loves to travel, cook, bike, and listen to live music, although usually not all at the same time.

Jenny Kalahar, a used & rare bookseller, lives in Elwood with her husband and pets in an old schoolhouse full of books. She is the author of three novels, *Shelve Under C: A Tale of Used Books and Cats*, its sequel, *The Find of a Lifetime*, and *This Peculiar Magic*. She also has published three collections of poems and stories, *One Mile North of Normal and Other Poems, All the Dear Beasties,* and *I Imagined a Dragon*. She is the treasurer for the Poetry Society and writes a twice-monthly humor column/blog in *Tails Magazine*. She helms Last Stanza Poetry Association in Elwood and is at work writing a fourth novel.

Casey Kenley (aka Punch Content) lives less than a block from Logan Street Sanctuary. She is a freelance marketing and writing contractor, mom to Leo and Ray, and wife of Polk Street Review co-founder Bill Kenley.

Bill Kenley is an English teacher at Noblesville High School and the author of *High School Runner (Freshman).* A five-time winner of NHS' Legacy Award, he was also the recipient of Indiana University's Philip Daghlian High School Teacher of English Award and a finalist for Indiana's Emerging Writer in the 2017 Eugene and Marylyn Glick Indiana Authors' Awards.

Jo Mader and her husband, John, have lived in Noblesville for nearly ten years along with an assortment of large dogs. The Farmers Market on Federal Hill is one of their favorite warm weather hang-outs. Jo has been writing for a number of years and is just getting involved again after an interesting round of medical episodes. She had work in the 2012 and 2013 issues of *The Polk Street Review* and is delighted to be able to contribute a new piece for 2018.

Gail Mehlan and her husband, Doug, are originally from the Chicago area. She and Doug love to spend time on their pontoon boat out on Morse Reservoir. They also love to travel and have visited Spain and Portugal. Gail is a wife, mother, grandmother and retired Bilingual/Spanish/English as a Second Language (ESL) elementary school teacher. Currently, Gail volunteers at the elementary school where her grandchildren attend in Noblesville and also for the Excel Center Childcare Center. She loves to sew and sews for the Indianapolis-based group called Little Angel Gowns. This organization turns donated wedding gowns into burial gowns for infants who don't have a chance to survive. Gail has taken several classes at the Indiana Writer's Center and is involved with a Faith Writing group. She currently writes sporadically for her blog, www.amongthesunflowers.blogspot.com.

Kurt Meyer is a co-founder of *The Polk Street Review* and author of the novels, *Noblesville*, and *The Salvage Man*.

Sally Meyer is a lifelong resident of Noblesville, a senior at Ball State University, and a contributor to the 2012 edition of *The Polk Street Review*.

Susan Hoskins Miller is a former journalist who has written for a multitude of newspapers, magazines and websites. Now she writes children's books and attempts to write poetry every once in a while. She has five grandchildren, who are her muses. She works in a university library and is the co-founder and board member of *Brick Street Poetry Inc.*, which brings poetry to people who might not realize how much they would love it.

Janet Moore, LMT, was a Noblesville resident from 1974 to 1993 and now lives in Westfield, IN with her husband, two dogs, and two cats. Janet's family moved to Noblesville in the winter of 1974 from St Louis, Missouri, when Noblesville was a small town, just a Single-A school. Janet remembers that era as a time when everyone knew each other and felt safe. Her family lived in the South Harbour subdivision, but Downtown Noblesville, where houses were quaint and unique, always called to Janet. After one year at Ball State University, the call of downtown Noblesville manifested in a 2/1 built in 1900. Janet was on the founding board of Noblesville Preservation Alliance; she says that it has been magical watching Downtown Noblesville restore. This edition of *The Polk Street Review* marks Janet's first submission to any publication. Her love for all of the arts has drawn her into dance, drumming, and painting. Watching creative expression emerge is spiritual to her. This spiritual connection extends to her work at Relax Adjust Zone, where Janet helps people relax, restore, and reconnect with themselves.

Sarah E. Morin serves as a kidwrangler at Conner Prairie Interactive History Park in Fishers, Indiana. She writes and performs unruly fairy tales and poems and is a regular performer at Fairyville at Nickel Plate Arts. Her first Christian fantasy novel, *Waking Beauty*, was published in April 2015. She is a member of American Christian Fiction Writers and a state officer of Poetry Society of Indiana. Sarah E. is the co-founder of *NICE* (Noblesville Interdisciplinary Creativity Expo), which saw its second successful year in 2016. She loved the years she spent living above the Clock Shop in Noblesville, and still remains engaged in the downtown scene through Noble Poets. (New poets welcome – 3rd Tuesday of each month at 6:30pm at Noble Coffee and Tea Co.) When she grows up she wants to be a child prodigy.

Crystal Morrison is an Airline Transport rated pilot and flight instructor. She has been flying for over 20 years and currently works in aviation management. Outside of the airport, her passion for rescue animals and writing takes the forefront. Her genre of choice include children's works and mysteries. She hopes to launch book one in her children's book series, *Adventures in Kibbletown* in 2018. Kiddos everywhere will get to meet BeBear and the Gang in the "Case of the Missing Biscuits" . Although a native Southerner, Crystal now reside in Noblesville, IN with her husband and small petting zoo comprised of three dogs and three cats.

Annie Oberman was born and raised in Hamilton County and has resided in Noblesville for the past ten years. She is the busy homeschooling mother of six children, ranging in age from 9 months to 10 years old. In her little spare time, Annie enjoys writing, drawing, painting, and photography. She is happiest when she is creating.

Kristina Oliver creates one-of-a-kind abstract art in her home studio near the arts district of historic Noblesville, IN. Her preferred media are acrylics and resin but she also works with pastels and alcohol inks. Kristina's main focus in the last two years has been in mastering different acrylic pouring techniques. She is completely self-taught. Kristina is a juried member of the Hamilton County Artists' Association (HCAA) and also serves on the HCAA Board as VP of Programming. She has solo/duo exhibited, as well as had individual pieces in galleries throughout central Indiana. Several of her paintings have placed top 3 in judged exhibits. Kristina's paintings are also part of private collections throughout the U.S. and Canada. She can be reached at: www.kristinaoliverart.com. More information about Kristina: kristinaoliverart@gmail.com.

Kid Quill is hip-hop artist, a graduate of Depauw University, and a lifelong Hoosier. His work can be found on iTunes, Spotify, and YouTube. He records his music in a private studio in Noblesville.

Greg Richards is in his 37th year as an English/Theatre Arts teacher at Noblesville High School. His inspirations and pastimes include literature, music, cycling, and indy films. He loves almost every aspect of his job and is a semi-regular contributor to *The Polk Street Review*.

Lorraine Rosio lives in southern Indiana. She grew up in Carmel, IN, and attended IU (Bloomington). Noblesville is the home of her best friend, and Lorraine is the godmother of her best friend's children. Lorraine says, "Thanks to my best friend, Noblesville has become a second home to me, a sanctuary, a respite from my daily life as my family's care giver. I look so forward to my days spent in Noblesville, walking, talking, and shopping downtown with my best friend. If it were not for those rare days, I often feel like there would be no joy in my life." Lorraine's submission to *The Polk Street Review* marks her first submission to any publication.

Ellen Santasiero's essays, memoirs, interviews, and articles have appeared in *Northwest Review*, *Marlboro Review*, *The Sun*, *Oregon Humanities*, *High Desert Journal*, *Oregon Home*, *Bend Living*, and *The Polk Street Review*. She teaches literature and creative writing at Oregon State University and memoir classes at private venues in Bend. Ellen is a 1979 graduate of Noblesville High School.

Mike Stewart is a life-long resident of Noblesville, arriving as a newborn at the Harrell Hospital in downtown Noblesville. He attended grade school at First Ward, junior high at the current Boys & Girls Club on Conner St., and was in the first freshman class to attend the high school built in 1961. After graduation, Mike played guitar and sang in several bands, performing in many of central Indiana and neighboring states finest dives. This halcyon time was interrupted by the US Army draft board. Though not his first choice, Mike was proud to serve his country for three years, including a one year tour in Viet Nam.

Mike is a retired Engineering Technical Designer. During his 46 years at HNTB, his many design projects included the Noblesville Sewage Treatment Plant. Glamorous, yes, but his true passion is his music, and retirement has allowed him to devote most of his time to playing guitar, singing, composing and recording his original songs, one of which is included in this year's *The Polk Street Review*. Mike generously devotes time to Logan Street Sanctuary, serving as a Board member for the all-volunteer organization.

Mike has two sons, ages 52 and 26 and 4 grandchildren. He and his wife, Sandy, reside in a Victorian home on Conner Street in Noblesville. The couple has renovated 3 historic homes together, relying heavily on Mike's carpentry skills. His latest project was designing and building a new screened area on the front porch of their Victorian home – without compromising the beauty and integrity of the structure.

Sandra Stewart, née Thacker, moved to Noblesville in 1952 at age five, a part of the hillbilly highway migration of southern workers to the Firestone Tire & Rubber plant. She attended grade school at Third Ward and First Ward schools, junior high at the current Boys & Girls Club on Conner St., and was in the first freshman class to attend the high school built in 1961. Sandy holds a BA from Indiana University, where she majored in fine arts with a concentration in figure sculpture.

After an early career in advertising and fashion retailing in New York and Boston, Sandy returned to Noblesville in 1982 and embarked on a thirty-five year career in elder services. She is the retired Executive Director of PrimeLife Enrichment but still serving the agency as part-time Development Director. Sandy is now a multi-media artist, in painting, sculpture, decorative arts, miniatures, needlework, or whatever strikes her fancy! She is delighted with Noblesville's transition from sleepy little town to charming destination city with a vital downtown area. Sandy and her husband Mike reside in their second Noblesville Victorian Home with their dog, Rumi. The Stewart's love their Conner Street home, built in 1889, and enjoy being able to walk to neighborhood restaurants, festivals and live music, especially at Logan Street Sanctuary! Sandy serves on the board of the Noblesville Preservation Alliance.

Maren Thornbury is currently a junior at Noblesville High School. She is a prolific songwriter and author, who, at the urging of her father, has finally decided to put some of her work "out there" and see what happens. Maren's submissions to the 2018 edition of *The Polk Street Review* are her first submissions to any publication.

Steve VandeWater has been a Noblesville resident since 1991, and has made a career in the concrete construction industry. Although he earned a degree in Fine Arts, his creativity has more recently been focused on writing. Steve's two favorite pastimes are drinking craft beer and playing the mandolin, but his wife Brenda would rather hear him drink the beer. The VandeWaters have three grown children, all of whom graduated from Noblesville High School.

Sam Watermeier was born into the entertainment world; his mother went into labor with him in a movie theater! He's been growing as a film fanatic, literature lover and journalism junkie ever since. Sam won the *Award of Merit* (Best of Book) for his memoir *Films About Ghosts* in the 2017 edition of *The Polk Street Review*. He got his professional start at *NUVO Newsweekly*, where he wrote movie reviews, filmmaker profiles and more from 2009-2017. Sam also contributes to *Midwest Film Journal* and Purdue University's *THiNK Magazine*. He's eager to write the same kind of fiction he marvels at on the big screen.

Mark Wilkinson is a native of Shirley, Indiana and has lived in Noblesville for over 30 years. His wife Cathy is a life-long Noblesville native, as are their children Zach and Emily. Mark is an educator with interests in IndyCar racing, Indiana University sports, and fastpitch softball. You can read more of his work at www.newtrackrecord.com.

Celeste Williams likes to say she is a native-in-law of Noblesville. She worked for 25 years as a journalist for daily newspapers in Indiana, Alabama, Tennessee and Wisconsin. Her first play, about appearances Frederick Douglass made in Indiana (highlighting the historical Roberts Settlement), was produced at Logan Street Sanctuary in Noblesville and at Conner Prairie in Fishers. She serves on the board of the Indiana Writers Center, and lives in Indianapolis with her Noblesville-native husband, Greg Fisher.

Spike Wilson Paul "Spike" Morin-Wilson is a professional director, actor, playwright, and designer. He holds a BA, MA, and PhD in Theatre, with an emphasis in directing, actor training, children's theatre, drama-for-literacy. He was the Director of the Kokomo Summer Drama Camp for 19 years, coaching over 1,000 students, ten of whom have had successful careers in professional theatre. He is a former teaching fellow for the Miami University Dept. of Theatre and the University of Pittsburgh Dept. of Theatre Arts, and a theatre professor for Ivy Tech Community College. He has 30 years of experience in the theatre, and has directed over 60 productions. Dr. Morin-Wilson currently serves as a Latin and Etymology teacher at Crispus Attucks High School and Head Speech Coach at Brebeuf Jusuit Preperatory School. He is proud to direct Page & Stage Theatre Co., a Logan Street Sanctuary Signature Event Series, which teaches theatre-for literacy through workshops, a summer camp, and soon, full-length productions.

Looking northbound, along Polk Street, Noblesville, Indiana
(photo by Alys Caviness-Gober)

About Polk Street, Grasshoppers, and Logan Street Sanctuary
Bill, Kurt, and Alys

In 1823, Noblesville was laid out and Polk Street, one of the main routes through town, was named after William Connor's partner, Josiah Polk. Polk Street is the north/south road now known as 8th Street, the one with a railroad track running alongside and down the middle of it. Mills once stood at Polk Street's north end, and it continued south, lined with the old Noblesville courthouse, bars, liveries, hotels, homes, and industry. For typical small-town-USA reasons, Polk Street/8th Street was a line of demarcation of "good" *v.* "bad" parts of town, blue collar *v.* white collar neighborhoods, industrial *v.* residential areas, and flood plain *v.* high ground. The street is often taken for granted, but it represents the history and lives of Noblesville and its residents. In 2010, Founding Fathers Bill Kenley and Kurt A. Meyer aptly name the first incarnation of *The Polk Street Review* in honor of a street so significant to Noblesville.

You may have heard us refer to the people who contribute to *The Polk Street Review* as "grasshoppers" and the people who quietly support them as "ants." These references hearken back to Aesop's fable, *The Ant & The Grasshopper*. Grasshoppers are the dreamers, the artists, writers, and musicians, the creatives among us. Ants are the people who support them, the hardworking in-the-background loved ones who take care of life's realities. Grasshoppers create that which inspires, that which feeds the soul; ants create that which feeds the body. The world needs both ants and grasshoppers, so cheers to both!

Logan Street Sanctuary, Inc. (LSS) is an all-volunteer 501(c)(3) nonprofit cultural arts organization. LSS offers regularly scheduled concerts, and arts and literature events, including our monthly *Second Saturday Songwriters Showcase* concert series, and our annual *NICE (Noblesville Interdisciplinary Creativity Expo)*, *Page & Stage Theatre Co.'s Summer Drama Camp,* and, since 2017, *The Polk Street Review* publication and book launch.

LSS' mission is to promote a greater awareness of and encouragement for Creative Arts in Hamilton County and beyond; to provide music, literature, and arts education, events, and exhibitions, which meet the interests of the community in general, and to encourage the arts in the community by providing diverse exhibits, events, and educational classes and workshops. *Logan Street Sanctuary, Inc.* hopes to establish high aesthetic standards and to cooperate with, and promote membership in, other similar organizations.

loganstreetsanctuary.org

www.ingramcontent.com/pod-product-compliance
Lightning Source LLC
Chambersburg PA
CBHW051102030726
47504CB00006B/1751